DEDICATION

To my wife, Connie, for always believing in me.

CONTENTS

ACKNOWLEDGMENTS

I want to thank my friends Gary Criner, Shayne Barker, and Miles Goosens (my unofficial editor); the staff of the microfilm room at the University of Kentucky library; the staff of the Archives Center, Public Records Division in Frankfort, Ky.; Mrs. Nell Pulliam; the nursing staff at the Louisville Masonic Home for Widows; the evening shift crew at the Danville, Ky. train station; George Flynn, Clerk of Pulaski Circuit Court, and attorney John Prather, both of Somerset, Ky.; Claude Decker, Jr. of Louisville, Ky.; Jack and Marlene Brown of Chattanooga, Tenn.; William Sandusky of Louisville, Alice Roof of Leitchfield, Ky.; Mrs. Gladys Fentress of Hardinsburg, Ky.; the staff of the McCreary County Record; the staff of the records room at *The Louisville Courier Journal*; and others in Whitley City, Ky. who wish to remain nameless. This book would not have been possible without the assistance of these individuals.

PREFACE

This book is a dramatic recreation of events which occurred in Kentucky during 1928 and 1929. It is based primarily upon newspaper accounts, limited available court documents, and interviews conducted in 1991 and 1992. Unfortunately, no transcript exists of the courtroom proceedings, and all of the key participants have been deceased for several decades.

I have reconstructed the trial from newspaper articles, using as a foundation the often substantial fragments of reported testimony. By utilizing as much as possible of the exact, reported words of each witness, I have strived to preserve the tone and content of each testimony.

All incidents and conversations prior to the incident on the train, with the exception of Pearl Owens' encounter with Rudolph Valentino, have been fictionalized, but even the fictional elements are closely based upon meetings described in trial testimony.

Several names mentioned herein are those of the actual people involved in the events described. I have used dramatic license in regards to describing physical characteristics and dialect for many of the supporting characters. Places, dates, and sequences of events are as accurate as could be discerned from available source materials.

CHAPTER 1

One candle flickered on a small circular table in the center of a sparsely furnished room. On opposing sides of the table sat a wrinkled old gypsy woman and Pearl, a dark-haired, twenty-five-year-old woman. With the fingertips of her right hand, the gypsy traced the life lines of Pearl's right palm.

"What do you see?" Pearl asked.

"I see that you have one child. A little boy," the old woman said. She retraced the same line. "You will have no more children."

Pearl smiled slightly with relief. She was proud of her five-year-old son, Robert, but one child was certainly enough. She loved the boy, but she doubted she would ever feel qualified or old enough to be anybody's mother. Both Pearl and Robert were fortunate; Pearl's older sister Annie was the mothering kind, and was overjoyed when Pearl placed Robert in her care. Pearl was confident that Annie would educate and raise Robert as her own.

"What else do you see?" Pearl asked.

"I see many things," the old woman replied. "You were divorced recently. Your ex-husband dearly loved you, and would have done anything for you, but he was unable to provide the material things you desire. Sometimes you miss the intensity of his devotion, but yours is a wandering heart, and you still haven't found who you are looking for."

"That's pretty much true," Pearl said.

"You have touched the hand of a great celebrity. He . . . is now deceased, but you feel he will somehow lead you to the man you are destined to love."

Pearl couldn't stifle the chill that came over her. One of her friends had told her about the uncanny accuracy of this old seer, but she had entered the shack with serious doubts about the woman's alleged abilities.

Pearl *had* touched the hand of greatness, just over three years ago, on April 1, 1923. That night, the great silent film star, Rudolph Valentino and his wife, Natacha Rambova, came to Louisville on one of the first stops of their promotional tour for the Mineralava Beauty Clay Company.

The actor was on strike from Paramount Pictures and his management company, Famous Players-Lasky Corporation, over artistic control of his future films. Valentino's current contract restrained him from acting or dancing for money for anyone else, but S. George Ullman, a public relations man representing the Mineralava Beauty Clay Company, found a loophole in the contract. Upon discovering that the contract did not exclude product endorsements, Ullman designed a promotional tour to take advantage of the film company's oversight.

Ullman organized a seventeen-week train tour of admission-free public appearances across America's heartland. At each stop, Valentino, dressed in a gaucho costume, and his wife, wearing Spanish attire, danced the tango he had made famous in his 1921 silent feature, *The Four Horsemen of the Apocalypse*. After each show, he called the audience's attention to his wife's beautiful complexion, and explained how Mineralava Beauty Clay had helped develop and maintain her lovely face.

Before each performance, Valentino was required to judge a beauty and a dance contest. When Valentino came to Louisville, Pearl and her dance partner, B. J. Coleman, were among the hundreds of dancers who performed for the actor under four huge spotlights in the Hawaiian Gardens.

The huge skating arena was filled with thousands of spectators and scores of dance contestants that night, and Pearl and B. J. danced flawlessly. When the contest concluded, Pearl was stunned to learn that the great Valentino had selected her and B. J. as the outstanding dancers.

Pearl was so excited she could hardly breathe when she came forth to accept her trophy, an engraved loving cup. The film idol bowed and kissed her hand before presenting her with the prize. Pearl stared deep into Valentino's dark eyes as he congratulated her and her partner. He was her ideal man. Pearl told herself that her life would forever be linked in some way with this dark, mysterious actor.

She had been to see Valentino in *The Sheik* more times than she could remember, but after meeting "the great lover" in person, all other men in her life paled in comparison. Like millions of women across America, she had dreamed of being abducted and romanced in Valentino's desert tent, but the reality of romance never measured up to its image on the silver screen. Still, Pearl insisted upon injecting her life with mystery and intrigue at every opportunity. She considered herself a free spirit, a sexually-liberated woman of the 1920s, and whenever she found herself in a man's arms, it was she who had chosen him, and she who decided how long she would be held.

Pearl had never lacked male companionship. Since her early days as a teen, young and old men alike had tipped their hats as she walked down the street. She was beautiful and sophisticated, and quickly learned the art of seduction and its rewards. She was twenty when she met young Elmer Owens, a struggling day laborer for a construction company.

From the day she said "I do," she knew she had made a mistake, but it was not one she suffered long over. For five years, she was the unworthy, solitary recipient of Elmer's love, but she knew many other lovers during their marriage. None of them were as unselfishly giving as her husband, but she was blind to his virtues. Instead, she kept looking for the man who could offer her the mystique of romance that Valentino had always promised on the screen.

Soon after her son, Robert, was born, she grew bored with the demanding, glamourless roles of wife and mother and began seeing other men. In the past three years, she had been in and out of several relationships with affluent men, with nothing more to show for it than a few pieces of cheap jewelry and a moderately-priced fur coat. Throughout all the nights in the Louisville and Lexington hotels, she had told herself that she was going to take acting lessons. She was going to save up enough money to make it to Hollywood, and someday she would look into Rudolph's eyes again, but this time the movie cameras would be rolling and the world would be looking on—

She never took acting lessons. Her dream of meeting her screen idol again never came to pass. Rudolph Valentino died of complications from stomach surgery on August 23, 1926.

Soon after her idol's death, Pearl decided to dissolve her unsatisfying marriage. She resolved to live her life as she imagined Valentino had lived his, free of any suffocating ties to home or family. She would go where she wanted, whenever and with whomever she chose, and feel no guilt for her deeds.

She divorced her loving husband, gave her little boy to her sister, and continued with the only life she had ever known. Her search for the ultimate romance continued in the speakeasies of Kentucky, Indiana, and Ohio . . .

"I see a man," the gypsy said. Pearl's attention returned to the flickering candle and the wrinkled old face across the table. "This man will have an intensity in his eyes that you will know instantly. He will be a quiet, distinguished man, and he will love you as you have only been loved once before. But unlike before, you will love him the same in return."

"Can you describe him for me? What does he look like?" Pearl asked.

"He has dark eyes, and dark hair, combed toward the back on both sides. He will have some form of physical disability, but it will not impair his ability to share life or love with you. "

"When will I meet this man?" Pearl asked.

"Soon. Very soon. You have passed by him before in a fine hotel in Lexington, but neither of you saw the other."

"What else do you see?" Pearl asked. "Tell me of our lives together."

"You will spend many passionate evenings together in various places. There will be some sort of connection between him and the celebrity you met, but I cannot see what it is. You will . . ."

The old woman grew silent, and a look of sadness passed over her face. "Yes, go on. Tell me more." Pearl demanded.

"I am afraid there are sometimes limits to how far I can see. This is all I can tell you."

The old woman rose from her chair, pulled the chain on a light fixture hanging from the ceiling, and returned to the table to snuff out the candle.

Pearl opened her purse, pulled out two quarters, and handed them to the gypsy. "Thank you," Pearl said. As her client walked out the door, the old woman forced a smile and said, "I wish you well." *You will need it, beautiful child.*

The old woman had seen more than she was willing to tell, but she had decided long ago that there were certain things which only seers and God should know.

CHAPTER 2

Within a month after leaving the fortune-teller's shack, Pearl found herself in a popular speakeasy across the street from Lexington's Grand Hotel. The city police were aware of the nightspot's existence, but it had never been raided, probably because several policemen were regular customers on their off-duty hours. Even out-of-state travelers knew about the joint's locally produced moonshine whiskey. The brew was as clear as a mountain stream and free of the deadly impurities which plagued what often passed for alcoholic beverages in the North.

When Pearl entered the bar, she saw a dark-haired, stoutly built man sitting alone in a secluded corner booth. As she gazed across the smoke-filled room, she could see that he was about ten years her senior. Impeccably dressed in a dark blue pinstripe suit, he sat with his left side facing the wall. All of the other tables and booths were taken, so she decided to walk over and ask to join him.

"Are you drinking alone?" Pearl asked.

"I hope not," the man said, smiling. He stood and offered her the bench on the opposite side of his table.

As she sat down, Pearl looked into his eyes; they were a dark, almost black shade of brown. There was something about the way he looked back at her that made her feel she had known this man for a long time.

"My name is Morgan," he said, offering Pearl his hand. "I'm in town on business."

"Pearl," she said, taking his hand. She noticed his palm and fingers were soft and uncalloused. "I'm visiting from Louisville."

"Have you been here before, Pearl?"

"A few times. Good watering holes are hard to find these days."

"Isn't that the truth. Prohibition makes it especially hard on the traveler. Can I get you something?"

5

"Yes. I'll have what you're having."

As Morgan raised his right arm to gesture for a waiter, Pearl saw that the left arm of his suit was folded and pinned at the shoulder. She had been so enchanted with the man's face that she hadn't noticed he was missing a limb. He had worked as a brakeman for the railroad during his early twenties, and had lost the arm while attempting to uncouple two coal cars. Morgan had never felt handicapped by his loss; his warm personality quickly put everyone he met at ease about the missing limb.

By the time Morgan had ordered the drink, Pearl recovered from her initial surprise and returned her gaze to his face.

"How long are you going to be in town?" she asked.

"Until Sunday afternoon. I finished up a series of meetings today, so this weekend is my time. Do you know where I could find a good tour guide for the city?" Morgan asked.

"I think I could be persuaded to show a gentleman around," Pearl replied. She returned Morgan's knowing smile. "By the way, what kind of business are you involved in?"

"I suppose you could say I'm in politics." Morgan was evasive. It had always been his policy to offer the ladies information in small bits; they always seemed to stay interested longer that way.

Pearl wasn't satisfied with his answer, but she knew there would be time later for more questions.

The waiter arrived and deposited Pearl's drink on the table.

"I hope you won't think I'm too forward," Morgan said, "but I'd like to propose a toast to you, Pearl. You are a most beautiful woman."

"And I will propose one to you, Morgan. You are a most charming gentleman."

The two joined their glasses, and just as the smooth whiskey touched their lips, the bartender shouted, "Last call."

Morgan placed his shot glass on the table and flipped open a large pocket watch. "It's only half past twelve," he complained to Pearl.

"That's usual around here," she said. "Lexington's finest like to have their whiskey in private after walking their beat. Nobody likes it, but at least it keeps the place open."

"No matter," Morgan said. He slid out of the booth. "I came prepared. I have a fifth of McCreary County's best corn squeezings back in my room. Would you care to join me?"

"I'd be delighted," Pearl said. She accepted Morgan's right hand and walked with him to his hotel.

They were sitting on the bed. Morgan's bottle was half empty when he decided to kiss Pearl. He leaned toward her, she met him half way. She wrapped her arms around his neck, ran her fingers through his hair, and they kissed like long-parted lovers.

The kisses grew longer and more passionate. Pearl removed Morgan's bow tie and unbuttoned his white shirt. With her arms back around his neck, she slipped off the bed and gently urged him to stand.

Morgan complied, and as he stood, Pearl removed his suit jacket and shirt. As she unbuckled his belt and pulled at his trousers, Morgan savored the novelty of having a woman undress him. His wife, Ina, had always waited for him to remove his own clothing, and although she usually granted his requests for sex, she had always avoided touching him anywhere near his amputation.

There had been other women during his marriage, but none had ever seemed as comfortable with him or as desirable to him, as this woman. Morgan delighted in the feeling of total acceptance.

After Pearl had undressed him and herself, Morgan became a different man. Like her beloved Valentino in *The Sheik*, Morgan stared deeply into her eyes and pushed her onto the bed . . .

All day Saturday and until after noon on Sunday, they remained in Morgan's room. Room service brought their meals, and all the while, Pearl fancied herself Morgan's passion slave. All her life, Pearl had resisted any man's efforts, be he father, husband, or lover, to control her, but in the separate world of the bedroom, she joyfully surrendered to her lover's every whim.

Pearl helped Morgan dress and pack for his trip home. He felt supremely satisfied, and although he had not yet admitted it to himself, he was falling in love with Pearl.

Pearl, wrapped in a sheet, sat on the edge of the bed and watched Morgan in the mirror as he carefully adjusted his clip-on bow tie with his right hand.

"I guess I didn't make a very good tour guide,"

"I would have to disagree with you there, young lady. There could never be a better one. Do you have a number where I could reach you, just in case I decide to see the sights in Louisville?"

"Sure. Get out your pen."

Pearl recited the number and address of her Louisville apartment. Morgan took it down on a small slip of paper that he placed in his shirt pocket.

"Well, I guess this is goodbye," Morgan said. He bent over the bed to kiss her. What he had intended as a quick peck grew into a long, tender kiss.

Just as Morgan turned the doorknob, Pearl said, "Do you have a number, where I can reach you?"

"I wish I did, but . . ."

7

That was ok. She should know better by now. Married men can't have strange women asking around for them.

"You're married," Pearl said, finishing his sentence for him.

"Who said anything about being married?"

"You didn't have to. I can sense these things."

"Does it bother you?" Morgan asked. He hoped his tone of voice would not reveal his genuine concern.

"Nah. All of the good ones are always taken, but I'm willing to share."

"I'll be seeing you," Morgan said. He hoped she would believe him.

"I'm counting on it." She wore a naughty smile. Morgan closed the door. Pearl secured the sheet around her and waited by the window to get a final glimpse of him as he entered a taxi. He didn't look up, but she knew he was thinking about her, and it wouldn't be long until they would meet again.

Morgan had always found it easy to hide the other women from his wife. Most of his encounters occurred on his bi-annual meetings of the Kentucky clerks of the circuit court. Twice each year, the clerks of each county's circuit court gathered in Louisville or Lexington for policy meetings. Morgan had always been content to enjoy the moment and forget the ladies when he got back home.

He tried to do the same with Pearl. He tried to bury himself in the grinding, daily routine of his job, poring over receipt books and balance sheets, but all his efforts failed. The way Pearl smiled, walked, talked, made love, haunted him night and day. Every moment, he found himself thinking of her.

Two weeks after returning home, Morgan stayed late after work. His heart raced as he finally found the courage to dial the number at Pearl's apartment.

After two rings, Pearl answered.

The sound of her voice intensified his memories of her, and the urge to see her again became unbearable.

"This is Morgan," he said. "How have you been, Pearl?"

"Missing you something awful,"

"Me, too, I'd like to come see you next weekend. That is—if you don't have any plans."

"Let me see." She paused briefly, then teased, "I think I can fit you into my busy social calendar."

The line was silent while Morgan pondered her remark. Had she been seeing someone since he left? He couldn't blame her if she had been. They never made any promises.

"You still there?"

"Yeah," he said.

"I have to work until five. After that, I'm yours for the weekend."

That sounded positive. At least he would learn where he stood with her.

"This Friday, six o'clock, your place," he said.

"Right. See you then."

One week later, Morgan told his wife, Ina, that he had been called away on business for the weekend. Ina accepted his story, and on Friday afternoon, he took a northbound train from Whitley City to Louisville.

When Pearl embraced him in the doorway of her second floor apartment over Longchamp's Millinery Shop, it was as if only seconds had passed since their farewell. Morgan was thrilled by the surprisingly familiar smell of her hair, and the soft, firm pressure of her lips against his. They made love throughout the night, and Morgan was surprised when an alarm sounded at 6 a.m.

"Sorry it had to be so early," Pearl shut off the alarm. "We need to slip out of here separately, if you don't mind. I don't want the neighbors talking."

"I didn't figure you for one who'd worry about gossip."

"I wouldn't, if not for Robert."

"You're married?"

"No, no. Robert is my five-year-old son. He's staying with my sister in Mississippi, but I don't want anyone talking to him about me when he comes to visit."

"Then you're divorced?"

"Legally, for about six months. We were separated for three years."

Morgan yawned, rubbed the sleep from his eyes, and reached for his trousers. "Why don't we talk about this over some coffee?"

Pearl accepted. She told him she'd meet him at a breakfast shop down the street. He dressed and left; she joined him a few moments later.

"Do you have any children, Morgan?" Pearl asked. She stifled a grin as she poked a fork through her eggs; this was the kind of question people usually ask before they jump into the sack together.

"Two girls," Morgan said. "Melissa is seven. Gloria's five."

"Your pride and joy, I'll bet."

"They're the only thing that keeps me married to their mother."

Pearl saw her opening and boldly rushed in. "Ever thought about leaving her?"

"Plenty of times. But I couldn't bear being away from the kids."

"You could visit."

"I want to be there for them. Part time wouldn't be good enough."

A dedicated father type. This was going to be tough.

"I didn't think I could be away from my Robert either, but once they get out of their diapers, it's easier than you think."

"Maybe for some people, but I don't think I could get used to it."

Morgan could see that Pearl was feeling him out, considering her future options with him. He returned to his meal and grew silent. Pearl knew she had moved too quickly, so she changed the subject.

"What are we going to do today?" Pearl asked.

"It's your town. What do you propose?"

"We have a trolley car that goes all over the city. We could take it to see the sights."

Morgan agreed, and they spent several hours window shopping in downtown Louisville. Pearl admired a pink silk dress and matching shoes in the window of a department store, and Morgan insisted on buying the expensive garments for her. That evening, Morgan waited across the street from Pearl's apartment as she changed into her new outfit.

After dinner in a fine restaurant, the couple went dancing. With Pearl by his side, Morgan felt younger than he had in the days of his youth. His desire for his beautiful companion was insatiable, and shortly before midnight, they checked into a downtown hotel; waking up to avoid the neighbors had not been to his liking, so Morgan didn't visit Pearl at her apartment again.

When Morgan left for the train Sunday evening, Pearl accompanied him to the station. Pearl knew from the look in his eyes that he was hopelessly in love with her.

Morgan stood on the steps of the train and said, "I'll be thinking of you all the way to Whitley City."

Pearl nearly fainted when she heard the name. "Did you say Whitley City?"

"Hadn't I told you before? It's a little town, about twenty miles south of Somerset."

Months ago, the old gypsy had told her that there would be a connection between the new love in her life and the celebrity she had met. Her beloved Valentino had owned a home early in his glory years in a section of Hollywood called Whitley Heights. A chill came over her. Whitley City— Whitley Heights. This was the connection to the great celebrity which the gypsy had foretold.

The train whistle sounded, and Pearl kissed Morgan goodbye. She smiled and waved at him as he took a seat by the window. Pearl was certain now that it was only a matter of time until Morgan would belong to her. Her destiny was being fulfilled.

Morgan called Pearl at least once each week from work. His life with Ina grew more difficult because she began to suspect his frequent weekend trips. In an effort to calm his wife's suspicions, Morgan began leaving work in the middle of the week for one-day, overnight "business" trips.

During the spring and early summer of 1927, he and Pearl often met late in the evening at the depot in Danville, Kentucky, which served as a middle-of-the-way meeting point between his home and Pearl's apartment. Morgan would leave Danville early in the afternoon of the following day, and to his wife's satisfaction, he would return to Whitley City in time for supper.

At least once every couple of months, Morgan managed to convince his wife that it was necessary for him to be out of town all weekend. On each of these weekend visits, Morgan brought Pearl an expensive gift. On one occasion, he bought a fur coat, and on another, a diamond set ring. Morgan was not a wealthy man by any means, but by cutting corners on his household expenses, he was able to make small monthly payments on his extravagant purchases.

Every time the couple met, they made love, but their physical passion was equaled by their spiritual love for each other. Each loved the other more than they had loved anyone before; Pearl rewarded his love by being faithful to him while they were apart, and Morgan showered Pearl with gifts to show his love.

CHAPTER 3

On the occasion of their first anniversary, the couple met and stayed again in the Lexington Grand Hotel. After entering their room, Morgan opened his suitcase on the bed and said, "I have a special surprise for you, Pearl."

"All of your surprises have been special, Morgan."

"This one is the most appropriate of all," Morgan said. "For the last year, you have been the most precious thing in my life, so I wanted to give you something that especially fits." He handed Pearl a jewelry box, which she quickly opened.

"A string of pearls!" she said. "Morgan, they're beautiful."

"Pearls for my lovely Pearl," Morgan said as she embraced him. After a few moments of intense kissing, they were making love.

The weekend, filled as always with fine dining, dancing, and loving, passed quickly. Sunday afternoon found the couple back in their hotel room. As Pearl helped Morgan pack, she found the courage to ask him the question she had wanted to ask since Friday evening.

"Morgan, did you really mean what you said the other night, about me being the most precious thing in your life?"

"Every last word of it." He was staring into his suitcase.

"Then why don't you show it? Divorce your wife and marry me."

"Pearl, I'd like that more than anything else in the world, but I can't. Ina might do something crazy."

"Like what?"

"Like kill herself. Several years ago, she shot herself when she found out I was seeing someone else."

"That would be her problem. What about us?"

No, that would be his problem. He didn't know if the girls would ever forgive him if he caused their mom to commit suicide. Hell, he didn't even know if he could forgive himself.

Pearl's heart ached as she waited for Morgan's reply. No matter what he says, he still feels bound to her.

She grew impatient, "You don't even know she would try that again. Maybe if you make her think divorce is her idea, she'll go for it."

"Any other woman would have given up on me long ago, but not Ina. It seems the worse we get along, the harder she tries to make it work."

"So, has she been succeeding?"

"I wouldn't keep coming back here if she had, would I?"

"I don't know. Some men like having their cake and—"

"Damn it, I'm not 'some' men. I thought you knew that by now."

"Maybe not. I know you're a very generous man, Morgan, but can't you see, you've given me everything except what I want most."

"But I'm giving all I can. We've got a good thing going. Maybe we shouldn't—"

"Maybe it's just good for you. I think we should spend some time away from each other. I know what I want. It's time you decided what matters to you." Pearl opened the door and gestured for him to go.

"Fine," Morgan said. He picked his suitcase off the bed and walked out.

Morgan endured the silence for two weeks before he phoned Pearl's apartment. When she heard his voice, she hung up. The following week, and once each week thereafter, he wrote her, imploring her to understand his point of view. She cried after reading each letter, but refused to write a reply.

Finally, after nearly two months, it became apparent to her that Morgan would not meet her demands. Pearl, unwilling to admit failure, convinced herself that she could live with the amount of time they had always had together; a two-day rendezvous each month was always filled with more love and passion than any other man could provide on a nightly basis.

The next time Morgan called, three weeks before Christmas of 1927, she was willing to speak with him.

"Pearl, we've got to talk. This thing's tearing me apart. I can't choose between you and my kids."

She wanted to say, "It's not a choice of me or your kids; it's choosing me or her," but Pearl bit her lower lip and said, "I know that. I'm not going to make you choose. I've decided I can live with things the way they were."

"Then you're willing to see me?"

"You name it," Pearl said.

"The diner near your place. This Friday at 6."

Early Friday evening, Morgan called to say that something important had come up which would prevent him from keeping their appointment. Pearl exploded when she got Morgan to admit that the "something important" was going shopping with his wife for Christmas presents for their children.

"I promise I'll make it up to you," Morgan said.

"How could you possibly make it up?" Pearl asked.

"By spending Christmas Day with you. Let's meet in Danville. From there, we'll go to the finest restaurant in Lexington."

There was a long silence on Pearl's end of the line. Then she said, "I suppose I can live with it. But I don't like it."

"Two weeks is a long time, but we'll make it worth the wait. I love you."

Again, there was a long pause. Finally, Pearl said, "I love you, too."

For the next two weeks, she kept thinking about Morgan out shopping with his wife, and the more she thought about it, the angrier she became. He was going to have to leave that woman, even if she had to help things along.

On Christmas Eve, Pearl dialed Morgan's home number. If he answered, she would tell him she was ill and would have to cancel their plans until the next week. If his wife answered, she would . . ."

A woman's voice said, "Hello."

"This is Pearl," she said. She was surprised by her own boldness as the words erupted from her mouth. "Tell Morgan that I'm mad at him and I won't be meeting him in Danville for Christmas." Then, acutely aware that her incriminating words could not be retrieved, she slammed down the receiver.

That evening, after the children had been put to bed, Ina asked Morgan who Pearl was. Morgan, as always, refused to discuss other women with his wife. She went crying to their bedroom, and Morgan went back to the office to call Pearl.

"Well, she knows about us now," Morgan said as soon as Pearl answered the phone.

"About time, don't you think? If you won't leave her, at least she's not going to enjoy having you. Maybe she'll see it's useless and give you a divorce."

"You had no right."

"Didn't I? Somebody had to do it, and lord knows it wasn't going to be you. Good night, Morgan, and Merry Christmas."

Pearl hung up before he could respond.

For the next six weeks, Morgan and Ina were like two strangers living in the same house. Ina rarely ate or slept, and was obviously in a state of deep depression. At the urging of her sister, Ina visited the family physician in Whitley City. After examining her, he sent her to a Lexington hospital for observation. The doctor in Lexington phoned Morgan in Whitley City to tell him that Ina would be hospitalized for at least the next week for treatment of severe depression.

Morgan was not surprised at the news. Since Pearl's call to Ina, his home life had been a living hell, and he spent all his time at the office thinking of Pearl. After a great deal of deliberation, he began to consider Pearl's point of view. She was right. He could not be responsible for what his wife might do to herself. Ina should accept that they could never be happy together.

For the first time since Christmas, Morgan called Pearl and told her of Ina's hospitalization.

"Looks like you knew what you were talking about. Do you want me to say I'm sorry?" Pearl asked.

"No. I've been thinking about what you said. Maybe it's time I stopped worrying about Ina. I want you to come to Whitley City and meet my girls. You can stay with us for a couple of days while Ina's away. I'll tell the kids you're an old friend of the family."

She accepted his invitation. Ina's children were impressed with Pearl's beautiful clothing and jewelry, and accepted her as their mother's friend. For the next two nights, after the children were asleep, Pearl slept with Morgan in the bed of her rival.

After Pearl returned to Louisville, Morgan entertained fantasies of leaving his wife. The children could grow to love Pearl, and they would enjoy living in two households. Everything could work out fine.

Morgan's fantasies were short-lived. Ina returned home, looking pale and more fragile than Morgan had ever seen her. Much to his surprise, he felt overwhelmed—with pity for his wife, and shame for his role in her decline. Then, to further complicate matters, their home burned in early March, and all of the family's possessions were destroyed. Morgan, Ina, and the girls moved into the Whitley City Hotel for a few weeks, then rented a house.

Throughout the hardships, Morgan remained in contact with Pearl. She was sympathetic to his plight, and patiently awaited the resumption of their affair. In May, Morgan received the insurance settlement on his house. With money in his pockets, he decided that Ina was well enough to care for the children in his absence.

On June first, Morgan attended the first of his bi-annual meetings of the clerks of the circuit court. The meeting, held in Lexington, marked the resumption of his weekends with Pearl. After they had checked into their hotel room, Morgan departed for a business meeting, leaving Pearl in the room to unpack. Just minutes after he had left, Pearl responded to a knock at the door. She cracked the door open just wide enough to see a petite, auburn-haired woman standing in the hallway.

"I'm looking for my husband, Morgan Simmons," she said, obviously surprised to be met by a woman. "This is his room, isn't it?"

"I wouldn't know, Madam. I am only the maid," Pearl said.

"Sorry to bother you," the woman said.

Pearl closed and bolted the door as her rival walked down the hall.

When Morgan returned from his morning meeting, Pearl informed him of their unexpected visitor. His face grew pale upon hearing the news.

"What did you say to her?" he asked.

"I told her I was the maid," Pearl said.

"Did she buy it?"

"She seemed to. I had the door cracked, so she didn't see anything more than my face. I've been afraid to set foot outside this door. If she saw me without a maid's uniform—"

"I didn't see her outside anywhere. Your answer must have satisfied her. She's probably gone on home by now."

"I hope so," Pearl said. "I don't want us to spend the weekend looking over our shoulders for her."

"This isn't like her. She's never checked up on me before. I'm not going to tolerate her—"

"Unless she brings it up, you're better off not mentioning it. How are you supposed to know she was here looking for you, unless 'the maid' made a special effort to tell you?"

"Guess you're right. Looks like I'll have to start making it a little harder for Ina to check up on me."

The next month, Morgan told Ina he had been called away for business in Tennessee, and then arranged a rendezvous with Pearl in the same Lexington hotel. After a passionate night, Morgan arose early the next morning. He was fully dressed when Pearl opened her eyes.

"I'm going out for a haircut," Morgan said. "How's breakfast sound, the diner across the street in one hour?"

"Fine."

Morgan left. Pearl dressed and walked down the stairs. She stopped on the mezzanine long enough to glance at the morning paper and smoke a cigarette.

Upstairs, an auburn-haired woman stopped knocking on Pearl and Morgan's door. Ina Simmons was both disappointed and relieved to find her husband's room empty. She had been trembling since leaving the depot. Ina had come to this city hoping to confront her husband and the other woman, and finally put an end to her agony; now it looked as if she might have to anxiously endure a long wait in the lobby for their return.

When she walked onto the mezzanine floor, Ina found herself behind a tall, dark-haired woman in a red satin dress. The distinguished-looking woman stopped and turned to extinguish her cigarette in an ashcan. Ina recognized the woman from her previous visit to the hotel—the woman who had been in her husband's room. This must be Pearl.

Ina followed her through the lobby and onto the street, all the while struggling to utter the woman's name. Finally, as the woman in the red dress prepared to cross the street at the corner of the block, Ina found her voice and called out, "Pearl?"

The woman turned to face Ina. "Yes. Do I know you?"

"No, but you know my husband, quite well in fact. I'm Ina Simmons."

Pearl responded with an amused smile that sapped Ina's small reserve of courage. Worse, she felt Pearl was staring at her plain gingham dress.

"Mrs. Simmons, I'm glad we finally meet," Pearl said. "What brings you to Lexington?

Ina was intimidated by Pearl's composure; she wasn't supposed to be so nonchalant about this meeting.

"My husband . . ." Ina began, and then stopped. She could feel the blood draining from her face. "He is here with you, isn't he?"

"Yes," Pearl said without hesitation. "He's stepped out for a hair-cut. He should be back in a few minutes."

"How can you be so at ease about being out with my husband?"

"He told me that the two of you were separated, that you weren't even living together anymore. Isn't that so?"

"It most certainly is not," Ina said, finally recovering a measure of the rage she had felt on the train ride to Lexington.

"Then it appears we've both been lied to, Mrs. Simmons. Let's go back into the hotel and talk about this."

Ina accompanied her rival to Morgan's room. Pearl removed a key from her purse and unlocked the door.

Upon stepping into the room, Ina's heart sank; Morgan's suitcase sat on the floor, alongside a pink piece of luggage. Pearl offered her a seat on the bed, then turned the desk chair toward the bed to face Ina.

"So, Morgan is still living with you?" Pearl lit a cigarette.

"He is," Ina replied, "and I'd appreciate it if you'd stop seeing him."

"Rest assured, Mrs. Simmons, as of today, we're through. I won't tolerate a man lying to me . . . Can I ask you one thing, Mrs. Simmons?"

"What's that?"

"How much money does Morgan make from his job?" Pearl, although always curious, had never asked Morgan about his finances.

"About a hundred dollars a month. Why do you ask?"

"Something's not right here. He spends more than that on me each month. See this dress, these diamond rings? He bought all these for me, and I've got a couple of furs in my closet at home."

Ina sat stunned for a moment.

Pearl noticed Ina's pained expression and broke the silence. "I'm not telling you this to rub it in."

Ina was not consoled.

Morgan was walking back to the room when he saw his wife and his lover standing outside the door.

"Morgan," Ina said. The coldness in her voice sent a chill down his spine. "Miss Owens has told me all about the stories you've been telling her. Our separation was real news to me. What do you have to say for yourself?"

Morgan stared at the floor and mumbled, "Nothing."

"I'm not surprised," Ina said. "It's been a long time since you've had anything to say to me. The fact that the three of us are standing here says it all."

She turned away from Morgan, looked at Pearl and said, "I forgive you, Miss Owens, for your part in this. I'm sure you wouldn't have had anything to do with my husband in the first place if he'd been honest with you."

"I promise you that Morgan and I are through, Mrs. Simmons," Pearl said. "We won't be seeing each other again."

"I'm glad. Now, Miss Owens, if you'll excuse me, I have a train to catch."

Ina turned her back on Morgan and Pearl and walked away.

Of course, Pearl could not keep her promise to Ina Simmons. She loved Morgan, and Morgan loved her; to Pearl, it remained as simple as that. Pearl felt his wife had no right to come between them.

The meeting in the hallway had dampened Pearl and Morgan's spirits, but as a matter of pride, Morgan insisted on spending the night with Pearl. He returned home to Whitley City on Sunday morning.

Neither Morgan nor Pearl had ever seriously considered ending their relationship. Their affair would continue, but they would have to be more discreet. The old meeting places were too risky. For August, they decided to meet in a different location.

August 9, 1928 found Pearl southbound on a train from Louisville. Morgan would meet her on the train when it stopped for passengers at eleven p.m. in Somerset. From there, they would travel to Chattanooga, Tennessee, where they would spend the weekend in a hotel. Morgan would bid her farewell late Sunday evening, and for the rest of the week, she would enjoy a reunion with her son, Robert, and her sisters, Annie and Nell.

As the train rattled down the tracks on the route from Louisville to Danville, Pearl passed the time by reading the latest issue of Vanity Fair. On the bottom of page 32, she read about Hollywood's latest femme fatale, a beautiful brunette named Evelyn Brent. "The fatal female," Pearl mumbled. She was proud she had once looked up the French phrase in a dictionary.

Pearl decided Evelyn was pretty enough for the movies, then turned the page. She would've been too—if she had made it to California. She had always used the same brands of makeup. Worn the same types of clothing. Had the same hairdos. Just never met the right people.

After Valentino awarded her the loving cup in '23, she had made a yearly resolution to save up enough money to make the trip to California. Every year, she ran through her meager earnings from working as a clerk in various Louisville jewelry and clothing shops; maintaining the 'Hollywood look' was a financially draining proposition.

Although the old familiar regret of a dream unattained still lingered, the articles in the movie magazines constantly reminded her that the directors were always looking for girls younger than she. In recent months, she had come to accept that her acting dreams were merely dreams. It was no great loss; she had always managed to manufacture sufficient drama for her real life, and gradually she accepted that movie audiences would never be looking on.

The train arrived at the Danville station at 10 p.m. Pearl and the other passengers disembarked. After a brief layover to change locomotives, new passengers from Danville joined those from Louisville, and they all boarded the No. 1 passenger train on the Queen to Crescent City route (Cincinnati to New Orleans).

For the next hour, Pearl grew eager to arrive in Somerset. It seemed an eternity since she last had embraced Morgan, and she was hungry for the sight of him.

Finally, the conductor announced the approach to Somerset. Pearl peered out her window and caught a glimpse of Morgan standing among the passengers waiting to board. In the months she had known him, Morgan had never been late for a meeting, but she always breathed a sigh of relief each time she saw him again, on time, waiting for her.

After some passengers disembarked and others began to board, Pearl stood from her chair near the center of the day coach and looked back, waiting for Morgan to enter. Upon entering the car, he immediately recognized her and smiled as he walked down the aisle. She moved to the window seat on the left side of the aisle, and Morgan sat down beside her.

Before saying a word to Pearl, Morgan glanced around the dimly-lit car to see if he recognized anyone. The two rows immediately behind them were vacant, save for a woman in a wide-brimmed hat slumped in her chair across the aisle. A few women and some children were seated in the back rows, but he didn't recognize anyone. Most of the seats in the front half of the car were occupied, but no one looked familiar from behind.

He longed to kiss Pearl there on the train, but Morgan had always been very discreet with their affair in public, especially when they were so close to his home. Somerset was the seat of Pulaski County, which adjoined his home county of McCreary. He had relatives in the Somerset area, and many people would recognize the one-armed clerk from Whitley City. Of course, there was no law against having a friendly conversation on the train with a charming young woman.

While the train took on coal and water, Morgan and Pearl discussed their weekend plans. As the minutes passed, it was Pearl who grew bolder, and at midnight, as the train pulled away from the station, she placed her right arm behind Morgan's neck. He still wanted to kiss her, but he resisted the temptation.

The train had traveled about a mile south of Somerset, and was just about to enter a little village called Ferguson. The car's lights were dimmed in respect for the lateness of the hour, and many of the passengers were napping. Pearl turned her head toward Morgan, and just as she was about to speak, something exploded in the car. Morgan watched in horror as Pearl snapped forward in her seat. Then, an instant later, the same deafening sound erupted again, and blood sprayed from Pearl's right shoulder.

Morgan and the other passengers immediately recognized the sound of gunfire. Men ducked down in their seats while women pushed their children to the floor and tried to cram them into the small spaces beneath the benches. Amid the screams and cries of the passengers, the conductor, Dan Dean, reached up and pulled the whistle cord. Immediately, the passenger train's brakes began screeching.

Morgan's ears were still ringing from the shots, fired at point-blank range from behind him. He turned and looked back after the second shot. There, with a 38-caliber revolver still smoking in her hand, stood a woman wearing a black dress and a wide-brimmed black hat. The clothing was unfamiliar, but he recognized the tormented face of his wife, Ina. Her gun was now trained on him.

A feeling of terror seized Morgan. He sprang from his seat and ran down the aisle into the next car.

Conductor Dan Dean looked at his watch as the train came to a halt. It was 12:05. Flagman John Heinz joined Dean at the center of the car. The woman in black, crying hysterically, had returned to her seat and placed the gun on the chair next to her. The conductor took possession of the gun while Heinz tried, unsuccessfully, to calm Ina Simmons. "You stay with her. I'll go call the sheriff's office," Dean told the flagman.

Within ten minutes, Patrolman McKinley Matney had arrived on the scene and placed Ina under arrest. He had taken statements from Dean, Heinz, Morgan Simmons, and several passengers who had heard the shooting. Matney was emerging from the train with Ina when Police Chief Robert Warren's cruiser pulled up with sirens blaring, followed close behind by a car driven by Gerald Griffin, a reporter for *The Somerset Observer*.

"What have we got here, Mac?" the chief asked.

"Looks like a jealous wife's shot and killed a woman that she seen sitting next to her husband."

"Anyone else hurt?" Chief Warren asked.

"No. Lot of folks scared out of their wits, but everybody else is okay."

"What about the murder weapon?" Warren asked.

"Thirty-eight revolver. The conductor gave it to the roundhouse foreman for safe keeping," McKinley said, pointing to the Ferguson railroad shop a short distance down the track. "Seems the lady was carrying it in a hatbox," He nodded toward Ina, who stood sobbing alongside the patrol car.

"She doesn't look in any condition to tell us anything," Warren said. "I'm going to take her to the courthouse, then have her admitted to Somerset General for observation. When you get finished here, come by to relieve me. I want a guard outside her door until they release her to us."

CHAPTER 4

As the police chief helped Ina into his patrol car, Morgan watched from a train window. Pearl's body lay on the opposite side of the aisle, now covered with a blood-soaked sheet.

Morgan stared as the car pulled away from the train with his wife in the back seat. His heart held neither sympathy nor anger toward her. Instead, he was filled with emptiness at the loss of the greatest love of his life, and a deep sense of guilt. He knew, from past experience, that Ina was capable of destructive, irrational behavior, but in the past it had always been self-directed. Tonight, Ina had done the unexpected, turned her torment outward, and Pearl Decker Owens was dead.

"Mr. Simmons, the hearse has arrived from the local funeral home for Miss Owens' body," the conductor said. "Will you be remaining on the train?"

"No," Morgan said. "I want to help with the arrangements."

Morgan disembarked. A local reporter, Gerald Griffin, was waiting beside the tracks. He introduced himself to Morgan and offered him a ride to the funeral home. As Pearl's body was loaded into the hearse, the men drove back into Somerset.

Griffin parked the car in front of the Somerset Undertaking Company, a two-story stucco building located one block down from the courthouse on the same side of the street. The lights were already on upstairs in the apartment over the funeral parlor, indicating someone had already called them to open for business.

"I know this is a terrible time to be asking, Mr. Simmons, but the press is going to be hounding you for your side of the story," Griffin said. "If you feel like talking to me, I could get a story on the wire service and maybe reduce the number of reporters who'll be coming your way."

"All right." Up until that moment, he hadn't considered the full implications of tonight's events.

The sight of Griffin removing a small pad and a pencil from his shirt pocket suddenly roused Morgan from the haze of his grief. He realized this wasn't private anymore. He would have to watch what he said.

"What was your connection to Miss Owens?"

"We were friends, just friends."

"How long had you known her?"

"I met Miss Owens in Lexington about twenty months ago, and we had been good friends ever since." Morgan paused, carefully considering his words. "I had seen her, not frequently, but from time to time. I saw her and liked her. She was a very beautiful young woman. I had not seen her for several months. There had been rumors about our friendship, and my wife heard these rumors and became jealous. She had caused trouble about it before."

"Did you know Miss Owens or your wife would be on the train?"

"No. I'd left Ina at work in the courthouse in Whitley City yesterday morning. I spent the whole day in Somerset on business."

"I've heard your name mentioned before. I understand you work in the courthouse in Whitley City?"

"Yes, I'm the clerk of the circuit court. I was elected to the office last November. Prior to that, I served two four-year terms as county court clerk. My wife serves as my chief deputy in the office."

"Why were you sitting beside Miss Owens?"

"I just happened to see her and sat down with her. She said she was on her way to Chattanooga to meet her sisters who were coming from Mississippi to meet her."

"You know that people are going to believe you planned to meet her on the late train?"

Another dangerous question.

"Any idea that my meeting Miss Owens was prearranged is ridiculous. I have a telegram here that Miss Owens received last Thursday from her two sisters, who, with Miss Owens' son, Robert, spent a few weeks in Oxford, Mississippi. She was showing it to me when . . . when Ina shot her."

"Did you see what happened?"

"When I heard the first shot I jumped up and glanced over my shoulder and saw it was my wife who was shooting. I brushed past her and beat it out to the rear of the train."

"Was Miss Owens dead at that time?"

"Yes, I'm sure she was."

"How did your wife know you or Miss Owens would be on the train last night?"

"It's a mystery to me. I don't know how she knew. And I'd never seen that outfit she was wearing before. If I'd recognized her, I would never have sat down with Miss Owens in front of her."

"Can you give me any background on Miss Owens?"

"She lived in Louisville. I think she was 27 years old. She was divorced, and had a seven-year-old son who lived with her sister, Annie Freeman." Morgan paused a moment to regain his composure, then added, "Pearl was pretty, so very pretty."

Morgan was distracted by the hearse bearing Pearl's body, which had just pulled up in front of the funeral home.

"I suppose I'd better go inside. If you need any more information, I'll probably be over at the Newtonian Hotel." Morgan pointed to the wide, columned front of the building directly across the street from the courthouse.

"I think I've got enough for the wire," Griffin said. He shook Morgan's hand. "I appreciate your help."

Undertaker O. W. Swain greeted Morgan at the front door, just after he had directed his employees in the hearse to take the body into the embalming room in the back of the building. Morgan introduced himself and explained that he would be representing Pearl's family in making arrangements for preparing the body for shipment back to Louisville.

He asked to be allowed to accompany the body into the embalming room, in order that he might recover any personal effects and valuables for safekeeping. Mr. Swain complied, and Morgan accompanied him into the embalming room.

Morgan wiped tears from his eyes as he looked at Pearl lying on the cold table. Mr. Swain lifted her hand and slid from her finger two expensive rings, one with a diamond set and the other with a ruby. Morgan had purchased the rings for her during the first year of their affair.

Swain placed the rings in a tray on the end of the long table, and then looked at Pearl's necklace. It was Pearl's favorite gift from him, and she had worn it proudly every time she had been out with him.

"Do you mind if I remove the necklace?" Morgan asked.

"No. If you wish, I'll leave you alone with her for a few minutes."

Morgan nodded his approval, and Swain left the room, closing the door behind him.

Morgan tenderly brushed Pearl's bloodstained hair away from one corner of her mouth, then traced his fingers across her lifeless lips.

"I'm so sorry, honey, that it's come to this," he whispered. "Better you'd never laid eyes on me. This isn't right. Dear God, this isn't right."

Morgan stood silent for a moment, all the while staring down at Pearl as if to make sure that, for as long as he lived, he would never forget a single detail about her face.

"I wish I could have buried these with you," Morgan said. He leaned over Pearl and carefully pulled at the string of pearls until the clasp faced forward. "But it's not for the rest of the world to know what you meant to me." He unlatched the clasp, and placed the necklace, Pearl's jeweled belt buckle, and the two rings into his handkerchief.

After placing the small bundle into the inside pocket of his suit coat, Morgan bent over Pearl and kissed her lips for the final time. Without looking back, he turned and walked from the room.

CHAPTER 5

By sunrise, it seemed the entire town had heard about the midnight murder. Even before normal opening hours, scores of curiosity seekers lined up outside the Somerset Undertaking Company in hopes of getting a good look at the body of the adulterous "city woman" who had been slain by one of their own country neighbors.

Undertaker H.C. Day peered between the curtains at the growing crowd outside the door.

"What do you see, H.C.?" his partner, Swain, asked.

"Hundreds of folks, mostly women, waiting for a look-see. You'd think they'd never seen a dead woman before."

"Least ways not one like this. This gal looked like a moving picture star."

"What do you want to do?" Day asked.

"Tell them to move her on into the viewing room," Swain said. "I don't see as it'll do any harm."

In the past, when victims had been run over by trains or mutilated in some other gruesome way, scores of townsfolk had flocked to the funeral home for a look. No one had ever complained about the practice or felt it improper, and no exception would be made with the body of this outsider.

After Pearl's coffin had been carried into the viewing room, the lid was raised, and the first of hundreds of people from the city and surrounding countryside began filing in to view her body.

Among the first through the door was an elderly farmer and his wife, who had arrived in town for supplies. The farmer paused for a long look at Pearl's face and remarked, "She sure was a pretty thing, wasn't she?"

"Yep," his wife said as she tugged on his arm to move him on past the coffin. "Too pretty for her own good. She should have knowed better than to come between a decent country woman and her husband."

Another man in the viewing line turned to undertaker Day and asked,

"Where was she hit, H.C.? Don't look like she's got a mark on her."

The undertaker explained that the fatal bullet had entered her brain from the back, and exited two inches above the left ear. Except for washing blood from her hair, Day said Pearl's face hadn't needed much preparation.

While hundreds of Somerset natives were satisfying their curiosity in the funeral parlor, Ina's relatives were busy searching for an attorney to represent her. Ina's brother-in-law, Randal Johnson, a traveling salesman, located his good friend, former state senator H. M. Cline, in the Cumberland Falls resort in McCreary County. Cline, a prominent attorney from Whitley City, agreed to represent Ina and accompanied Johnson in his car to Somerset.

Cline met with Ina in Somerset General Hospital and prepared her for the arraignment. By this time, Ina had regained her composure and was primarily concerned about being reunited with her two daughters. She had left the children with her parents in Junction City, a small farming community near Danville. Cline promised Ina he would have her daughters brought to her as soon as more comfortable arrangements could be made.

Upon leaving the hospital, Cline went to the courthouse, where he met with Chief of Police Robert Warren. The attorney explained that Ina's daughters would be greatly distressed upon hearing of the arrest of their mother, and that the three of them should be reunited as soon as possible. Warren replied that the county jail was not equipped for female prisoners, and that he sympathized with the children's plight.

The chief called his wife, and she agreed with him that Ina and her daughters could spend Friday night in the Warren home. Ina was scheduled to appear before County Judge Napier Adams at 10 o'clock on Saturday morning for arraignment.

From the courthouse, Cline proceeded to the Newtonian Hotel to interview Morgan concerning the case. By this time, Morgan was weary from his sleepless night, and refused to provide Cline with anything more than the brief statement he had given the police on the train.

As Cline walked outside, he was met on the hotel steps by newspaper reporters from as far away as Louisville and Lexington.

"What did Mrs. Simmons tell you?" one of them asked.

"Mrs. Simmons told me that she was on the train looking for her husband, who had been spending a lot of time away from home," Cline replied. "She didn't say she knew that Miss Owens would be on the same train, but I believe she had such information."

"How did she find out Miss Owens would be on that train?" another reporter asked.

"She didn't tell me how she knew," Cline replied.

"Why did she shoot Miss Owens?" Gerald Griffin asked, busy updating his earlier wire story.

"She hasn't admitted to shooting anyone, gentlemen. Mrs. Simmons merely said the woman was breaking up her home, and that she had caught them together twice before, in Lexington."

"And what did Mr. Simmons say about that?"

"I'm afraid Mr. Simmons wasn't very forthcoming with me a few moments ago when I interviewed him."

"Do you think your client was justified in shooting Miss Owens, if what she told you is true?" Griffin asked.

"I'm not going to speculate on such things," Cline said. "That's all I can tell you for now." Cline stepped into Randal Johnson's car and rode with him back to Whitley City.

The evening edition of *The Louisville Courier* contained the updated version of correspondent Gerald Griffin's account. At three o'clock Friday morning, Griffin had called Miss Maude Long, proprietor of Longchamp's Millinery Store, at 713 West Jefferson Street in Lexington. Miss Long, identified by Morgan as Pearl's landlord, told Griffin that Pearl had occupied an apartment on the second floor for a month, but she knew nothing more about her, and was unaware that Pearl had left the city.

A staff reporter in Louisville interviewed Dr. J. T. Windell, the owner of the adjoining building on 715 West Jefferson Street. Dr. Windell told the reporter that Pearl had occupied different apartments during the past two years. Two months prior, she had rented an apartment on the second floor of the Longchamp's Millinery Store. He said he didn't know anything else about Pearl.

When interviewed later, occupants of the third floor of the building were also unable to provide any information about Pearl's habits, family, or friends. Several residents said they had tried to be neighborly when they saw Pearl in the hall, but her conversation had never extended beyond a polite 'hello.'

The truth was that Pearl had never felt comfortable around other women; she felt her peers all envied her beauty, and older women were likely to criticize her bohemian lifestyle. With the exception of her former dance partner, B. J. Cole, she had had no platonic male friends, and had seen few benefits in forming such relationships.

By 6 p.m. Friday evening, Pearl's coffin had been packed into a crate and loaded onto a train bound for Louisville.

Morgan accompanied the body on the train, and during the long ride, he had time to assess his life. A part of him had died with Pearl, and he felt terribly alone. He blamed himself for her death, and every time he tried to remember the times they had made love, his memories returned to the sight of Pearl lying pale and lifeless on the undertaker's table.

Pearl had been so vital, so fresh and alive, even childlike for her age, and now she was no more. Even in his memories, he could not return to his joyous days with her.

What about his children, Melissa and Gloria? He decided they would still love him, but would they blame him later for hurting their mother so deeply that she felt compelled to commit the ultimate crime? How would they react if their mother received the death penalty or life in prison?

He dearly loved his girls; that was the only reason he had stayed in his marriage. He decided on the train that he would do everything he could to redeem himself in their eyes, even if it meant he had to work for Ina's acquittal.

At 9:35 p.m., the train arrived in Louisville. A hearse was waiting to take Pearl's body to the John Mass & Brother funeral home. Morgan presented the driver with Pearl's death certificate, and then hailed a taxi as the hearse drove away.

From a phone in the lobby of the hotel he had chosen for the night, Morgan called Pearl's brother, Noah, to tell him that he could take possession of Pearl's body. Noah had never spoken to Morgan prior to Pearl's death, but he had heard their sister, Nell, say something about Pearl "messing around with a married man."

Noah assumed Morgan was that man, but he didn't speak of this, and in his heart he held no animosity toward him. He politely thanked Morgan for all the arrangements he had made in Somerset, and told him that Pearl would probably be buried alongside her late father, Lawson, in Glen Dean, Kentucky.

Noah briefly reminisced on the phone about several things he would repeat for the reporters who would gather outside the Mass Chapel the next day. Pearl had moved in with Noah and his wife soon after their mother died in 1915. She had lived with him until shortly before her marriage to Elmer Owens.

Seven-year-old Robert was the only child to result from the marriage. Noah said he believed Pearl's sister, Annie Freeman, would probably adopt the boy and give him a good home and an education, things which Pearl had not been secure enough to provide.

Pearl, of course, had told Morgan most of these details, but he politely listened to her brother review her life. After Noah finished speaking, Morgan told him how sorry he was about what his wife had done. Morgan was relieved when Noah accepted his apology. Noah said that Pearl's other brothers and sisters weren't terribly surprised that she had come to such an end.

"She was always such a stubborn girl," Noah said. "Nobody could ever talk her out of a notion once she got it into her head. She was always restless. She spent a lot of time going to the picture shows. I guess real life never was good enough for her. Lord knows Elmer, her poor husband, tried to give her everything to satisfy her, but seems like it was never enough. She was always looking for something, but I guess she never found it."

"I suppose not," Morgan said, just before hanging up. No need to tell him the whole truth. Morgan believed Pearl had found contentment with him, but his wife had staked a prior claim, and defended it with deadly force.

CHAPTER 6

Ina was scheduled to appear before Judge Napier at 10 a.m. on Saturday, but a crowd began forming outside the courthouse before eight o'clock. Acts of violence by women were not rare in the region, but the fact that the victim was from "the big city" had added immensely to interest in the case. As the hands on his pocket watch approached ten, Judge Adam Napier looked out a front window of the courthouse at the ever-growing crowd. Patrolman McKinley Matney, who had just entered the building, approached the judge.

"What are we going to do, your honor?" Matney asked. "They must be over a thousand people out there, more than half of 'em women. The county courtroom won't hold but 250."

"Tell them we'll have the hearing in the circuit courtroom," Judge Napier said. "It'll hold at least twice as many. If you have to, let some of them stand in the aisles. And send someone outside to explain to those who don't make it in. Last thing we need is a riot on our hands."

After the circuit court room had been prepared, more than 500 spectators filed in. When all the seats had been filled, people were allowed to crowd into the aisles and line up against the three walls opposite the judge's bench. The last spectators to be admitted perched on the bannisters that separated the audience from the tables for the defense and the prosecution.

Shortly after 10 a.m., Ina entered the courtroom from a rear entrance, escorted by her two daughters, a brother, Albert, and her father, Chris. Illness had prevented Ina's mother from accompanying Chris when he brought Ina's daughters to Somerset Friday afternoon. The children, along with their grandfather, had joined their mother at Police Chief Warren's house, where she had spent Friday night under house arrest.

After Ina's group had been seated, they were joined by H. M. Cline and

Somerset attorney W. Boyd Morrow, brother of former Kentucky Governor Edwin P. Morrow. Cline had enlisted the local attorney late Friday evening in hopes that Judge Napier would look more kindly upon Ina's bail request if it were delivered by a familiar face.

At the hearing, Ina waived preliminary examination on the murder charge, and Judge Napier ruled that she be held under $5,000 bond to the Pulaski County grand jury, which would hear the case on October 2, 1928.

Morrow presented the bond, which was provided by George Hatfield of Whitley City, Ina's father, Chris Cummings, Dr. W. R. Cardin of Somerset, and James Pinnell, also of Somerset. With the drop of his gavel, Judge Napier adjourned the hearing, and more than two hundred spectators, most of them women, rushed toward Ina to offer her best wishes and hopes that she would be exonerated at her upcoming trial.

"God bless you, Ina," one middle-aged woman said. She embraced Mrs. Simmons as she walked out of the courtroom behind a police escort. "You gave that tramp what she deserved," another woman in the aisle said.

As she continued from the courtroom, Ina shook every hand offered her and returned the many smiles of her admirers. When she emerged from the courthouse doors, she was greeted by the applause of hundreds of spectators who had waited outside for news.

Ina felt vindicated by the approval of so many decent, God-fearing country folk. She felt all of them were just like her. They worship God, stay at home, raise their families, and mind their own business. If someone had tried to steal their husbands or wives, they would have done the same as she.

Newspaper reporter Gerald Griffin stood just below her on the courthouse steps.

"Is there anything you would like to say to our readers, Mrs. Simmons, and of course, to the folks here?" Griffin asked.

"Yes," Ina said. She stood with her six-year-old daughter, Gloria, clinging to the left side of her dress and nine-year-old daughter, Melissa, nestled under her right arm. The perfect picture of motherhood. Griffin would later suggest this same pose to the photographer in the Somerset Photo Studio when Ina posed for a picture for the newspapers. "I want to thank the officials of Somerset for the kindness they have shown me, especially Chief Warren and his dear wife, who allowed my children and I to spend last night in their home. I also want to thank all of you here today for standing beside me and my girls in this time of trouble. I thank God for each and every one of you."

The adoring crowd cheered and applauded Ina's remarks, and Ina acknowledged them with a smile.

"Mrs. Simmons," another reporter shouted from the throng at the bottom of the steps. "Your attorney stated yesterday that Miss Owens had been tearing up your home. Could you tell us more about what had been going on between your husband and Miss Owens?"

"I'll tell it all at my trial," Ina said, offering the only response she would give to the reporters and other curious individuals she would encounter in the coming months.

Attorney Boyd Morrow stepped in front of his client and said, "That's all the time we have for questions today, boys. Mrs. Simmons has an appointment to have her picture taken for the papers."

Ina and her family members followed the police escort down the courthouse steps. Scores of people from the crowd walked alongside her all the way to the studio, happy for the opportunity to shake Ina's hand and wish her well.

While Ina was being photographed for the evening papers, Morgan was in Louisville being interviewed by a *Louisville Courier-Journal* reporter. Pearl's brother, Noah, interviewed earlier by the same reporter by telephone, had disclosed where Morgan was staying.

Morgan accurately repeated most of the details he had given Gerald Griffin the day before, but he had had time to read the wire account in the evening papers, and decided to amend his story. Earlier, while sitting in the car with the reporter outside the funeral home, he had stated that, after seeing the smoking gun in his wife's hand, he brushed past her and ran out of the car, fearing she would shoot him next. Today, he told the Courier-Journal reporter that he had been misquoted in the earlier newspaper story.

"My wife had no intention of shooting me," Morgan said. "She put the gun down on the seat she was standing next to, and the conductor picked it up after the train stopped."

His wife had committed a cold-blooded murder, which was bad enough. There was no need to perpetuate the idea that Ina had gone totally out of control. This woman was, after all, the mother of his two sweet young daughters; it would not look good in the press if it appeared she had been willing to murder their father for merely sitting beside a pretty young woman. A jealous mother might murder the woman she perceived to be wrecking her happy home, but she would never kill her husband; without a husband and father, there would be no home to defend.

Later, Morgan read his words in the Saturday evening paper, which appeared exactly as he had spoken them. He had taken the first step toward getting back into his daughters' lives, but he knew there was more he could do. He only prayed it would be enough.

CHAPTER 7

On Sunday morning, Morgan got up early and read the newspapers. He learned that Ina had been released on bond, and would be staying with her parents in Junction City.

He expected her stay there would probably be brief. Ina and her mother differed in their opinions over housekeeping, and it would only be a matter of days until Ina would be ready to return home to Whitley City. In the meantime, Morgan would take advantage of the opportunity to return to the house and remove all of his personal possessions. He reasoned that Ina would be more likely to bring his girls back home if she knew Morgan had moved out.

Sunday evening, he boarded a train for Whitley City. As the train neared Danville, he was torn over whether he should get off at the station and call to ask for permission to see his children.

The train finally arrived in Danville for a brief layover at the depot. While he waited, Morgan stared long and hard at a telephone. Since it was Sunday, Ina's farmer father, Chris, would probably answer the phone, and Morgan could anticipate the response he would receive. He walked past the phone and boarded his train.

When he arrived at his home in Whitley City, Morgan packed his clothing and a few pictures of his daughters. He intended to spend the night in the house, and then look for a room at the Whitley City Hotel, where he and his family had briefly stayed after their home had burned. He knew the girls would enjoy their visit with their grandparents, but he felt it would be best for them to return to their own home as soon as possible. As soon as Ina received word that he had removed his belongings, she would probably come home.

On Monday morning, after he had checked into his hotel room, Morgan walked down the street to the offices of his wife's attorney, H. M. Cline.

Cline's secretary ushered Morgan into the room.

"Have a seat," Cline said, pointing to a high back leather chair in front of his oak desk. Cline didn't offer his hand to Morgan, and was still clearly displeased that Morgan had been so stingy with details about the shooting on the train.

"What brings you here this morning, Mr. Simmons?" Cline asked.

"I want you to tell Ina that it's all right for her and the girls to come back home. Tell her I moved all of the stuff that I cared to take out last night, and I won't be around to bother her between now and the trial date."

"Is there anything else?"

"I would like to see my daughters,"

"That may take some doing," Cline said. "Ina didn't give me any clue on how she felt about the girls seeing you. I'm sure the children are pretty much in the dark about this whole matter, unless someone has been talking to them."

"I'm sure their grandmother has been giving me the blame for all of this."

"Speaking frankly, Mr. Simmons, you do share a sizeable amount of the blame, don't you? You put your wife through pure hell over this Owens woman. And she tells me that the Owens gal wasn't the first. Your entire association with your wife has been marked by infidelities. Lord knows how the poor thing stood it as long as she did."

Morgan didn't respond to the allegations. He did feel responsible, to a large degree, for the crime which Ina had committed. He should have been more considerate of Ina's feelings, but all he had been aware of before he met Pearl was his own emptiness. That same emptiness had led him into the arms of other women earlier in his marriage.

"I . . . want to help with Ina's defense in any way that I can," Morgan said.

"She's going to need all the help we can get if we're going to keep her out of the electric chair. I read the Louisville papers this weekend. You changed your story a little bit about whether it looked like Ina had you in her sights."

"Just between you and me, Mr. Cline, when I was looking up the barrel of that gun, I believe she did want to kill me. But I don't want them to kill Ina for what she's done. The girls need their mother. Maybe the jury will have some pity on her if it looks like she was trying to keep Pearl from taking me away from her. But how would it look if she wanted to kill both of us? They may think she wasn't concerned about keeping us together as a family."

"I see you've been thinking along the right lines; you want to help Mrs. Simmons. Kentucky law says you can't be forced to testify against your wife. You could testify for her, but I'm afraid that any testimony you offer could be used against her. I don't believe it's in your wife's best interest to use you on the stand, but there is something you can do. There's a lot of leg work to be done, and it's going to take a lot of time."

"I'm willing to do whatever I can."

"You'll be helping paint an ugly picture of yourself."

"That doesn't concern me. I don't have any control over what people are going to think or say about me. That's not what's important anyway. Ina and the girls are what matter now. They're all that matters."

"All right then. I've been thinking about a possible strategy. We're going to have to build our case on insanity, show the jury that over a period of years, you drove Ina to the brink. Ina told me she's been in and out of at least half a dozen doctors' offices since you first started going out on her.

"All of those doctors will have your wife's medical records and be able to attest to her mental and physical state through the years. Our only hope may be that their testimony can provide a picture of her mental and spiritual deterioration from the torment you and your lady friends were putting her through. Your job will be to visit all those doctors' offices between here and Lexington. Convince them how important it is to Ina and her babies that they come down here to testify. I'm sure they'll appreciate it if you offer a little transportation money for their trouble."

"I'm willing to go wherever I have to," Morgan said.

"Good. Here's a list Ina gave me of every doctor she's been to see since she married you. You'll probably remember where most of them practice. The quicker you can start the field work, the sooner we'll know where we stand with this defense."

Morgan used his one hand to fold the list against the table, and then slipped it into his pants' pocket. He offered his hand to Cline and said, "I'll get started on this today."

"I'll count on it then." Cline showed Morgan out of his office.

In the evenings after work at the McCreary County Courthouse, Morgan made personal visits to the homes and offices of all the doctors on the list Cline had provided. Each of the doctors expressed their concern for Ina and promised they would gladly testify regarding her physical and mental health through the years.

On the way to his hotel room each evening, Morgan walked past the rented house he and Ina had lived in for the months preceding Pearl's murder. Every day, he looked into the windows, hoping for a glimpse of his daughters, but each time, the place appeared as deserted as it had on the day he had removed his clothing.

After two weeks had passed, Morgan returned to Cline's office to inquire about his request to see his children. Cline told him that Ina had decided it was best that she and the children remain at her parents' home in Junction

City, and that she didn't want Morgan to see his daughters until after her October trial. In reality, the children had moved back to Whitley City before the beginning of the fall school term. While their mother remained in Junction City, the children lived with a neighbor across the street from the lot where their home had burned the previous winter.

Days prior to the October trial date, Ina and her attorney were given additional time to prepare her case. Commonwealth attorney Jacob Schuyler (pronounced Skyler) Sandusky, who had been assigned to prosecute, filed a motion for continuance on the grounds that several witnesses for the prosecution could not attend the trial on the proposed October 2 starting date. Sandusky's motion was granted, and the trial was reset to begin on February 14, 1929.

CHAPTER 8

Early in December, nearly two months before the trial date, Sandusky offered a young Mount Vernon attorney, Howard H. Denton, the opportunity to assist with the prosecution. Denton, not yet twenty-five, had recently graduated from law school, and arrived in Kentucky from Madison, Indiana. This case would be Denton's first murder trial.

Sandusky, a native of Monticello in neighboring Wayne County, and his wife, Clara, had instantly taken a liking to young Denton, and allowed him to live for a time in their Monticello home. Later, Mrs. Sandusky would introduce the previously-married Denton to the Somerset librarian, Miss Grace Propst, whom he would eventually wed.

The forty-eight-year-old Sandusky was a well-known, experienced trial attorney. Later in his career, he would be elected circuit judge (1934-46), with jurisdiction over five districts, and be seriously considered as a Republican candidate for governor.

Sandusky stood 6' 2" and walked with a pronounced limp. As a youth, while working on the family farm, a hay wagon had rolled over his right foot, and a life-long limp developed. Despite his injury, he enjoyed taking a long walk each evening, and maintained impressive upper body strength from chopping wood. Although his duties for the commonwealth kept him extremely busy, he found time for quail hunting and was considered a great marksman. At the First Baptist Church in Monticello, and later, at a church bearing the same name in Somerset, he served as a deacon.

Howard Denton was in the commonwealth attorney's second-floor Masonic Building office early on a December morning for his second conference on the murder case. Howard rifled through a stack of legal pads as Sandusky asked questions from the opposite side of his desk.

"Did you get in touch with Miss Owen's relatives?" Sandusky asked, going down a list he had prepared.

"I got calls through to her brother, Noah, in Louisville, to one of her sisters in Mississippi, and to her sister, Nell, in Indianapolis. None of them plan to press charges or attend the trial."

"That's odd. Most people would be outraged that their sister had been so brutally murdered."

"I think they're more ashamed than outraged. They seemed disgusted that their sister had been caught carrying on with a married man."

"Did they know about her relationship with Morgan Simmons?"

"Not very much. Pearl had told Nell something about seeing a married man who held some kind of political office, but she hadn't named names. Mrs. Pulliam scolded her for it. So did her brother, Noah, but apparently Pearl had never been one to take advice. The word that comes up most often when they talk about her is headstrong. Once she set her mind on something, nobody and nothing was ever going to change it."

"Until Mrs. Simmons came along with her pistol," Sandusky said.

"Pearl's mother died when Pearl was sixteen or seventeen. She was too much for her father to handle, so she moved in with her brother, Noah. She stayed with him until she met and married Elmer Owens. According to Noah, Mr. Owens was very demonstrative of his love to Pearl, but he was unable to provide the material things she wanted, or get her into the better social events."

"The papers said something about a seven-year-old child?"

"Yes. They had a son, Robert. I spoke to Elmer Owens yesterday. He said he had signed papers giving Pearl's sister, Mrs. Annie Freeman, permission to adopt Robert."

"I would like for the child to attend the trial, to let the jury see that Pearl has left someone behind."

"Mrs. Freeman said the family didn't want to get involved in any quote, 'trashy scandal,' unquote, and that Robert had suffered enough."

"I can't really blame her," Sandusky said. "But it's going to be mighty hard to compete for the jury's attention. I imagine that Ina will have her two little girls sitting beside her the whole time during the trial. On the one hand, the jury is going to be asked to sentence those little girls' momma to the electric chair. On the other hand, you have a little boy's mother who has already been executed and planted in the ground."

"But without some flesh and blood relative in that courtroom, the jury will be dealing with an abstraction," Denton said. "Pearl Decker Owens will just be a name to them, someone who had come between a short, petite little woman and her right to a happy home."

"We have to hope that the evidence for cold-blooded murder will outweigh the jurors' natural sympathy for Mrs. Simmons' children. I think we have a good case. There doesn't seem to be any doubt as to who pulled the trigger on that train," Sandusky said.

"What if establishing guilt isn't enough?" Denton asked. "It seems like everybody in town thinks Pearl got what she had coming to her. In law school, one of my professors used to say that sometimes the best thing that can happen in a trial is to be tried by a jury of your peers, people who hold the same prejudices and values—narrow-minded as they might be."

"Maybe establishing guilt won't be enough to convict, but that's our strategy going in. If it looks like it won't work, we'll have to adjust our case accordingly. Murder trials are usually a give and take thing. The way we open may not have any resemblance to the way we have to close. Now, for the next item," he said, looking down his list. "There have been rumors, probably started by Ina's family, that Morgan Simmons was indicted last June for embezzling from McCreary County through his position as clerk of the circuit court. Anything to it?"

"I made a trip to the McCreary County Courthouse and looked through the indictment files since Simmons was elected to his current job. There was nothing about any indictment involving him, nor did anyone in the courthouse seem to know anything about it."

"I'm not too surprised," Sandusky said. "You'll soon learn that Kentucky politics in general, and McCreary County politics in particular, are, to put it politely, less than aboveboard. I don't have any doubts that his wife's rumored accusations are true. After all, she worked in the same office with him. I also don't have any doubts that someone in the courthouse has taken steps to protect their own. Their records, like ours, are mostly hand-written. It's not too huge a task to rewrite a few pages or lose a document."

"How do you think the embezzlement fits in?" Denton asked.

"Here's the way I figure it. Miss Owens developed a taste for nice things and rich nights out. Simmons found himself strapped for cash, and dipped into county funds to supply her with furs and jewelry. After he was indicted, he tried to cut out the goodies, but she wouldn't let him. Pearl Decker Owens became too big a burden, so he arranged for her murder."

"So you believe he put his wife up to it?" Denton was stunned. "Why would she take such a chance?"

"He must have let her know that he had planned a meeting with Miss Owens on the train. How else would his wife know to be on the same train at the same time with them?"

"But he and his wife should have known that she would get the chair for it. And she did it in front of a carload of passengers, so—"

"So she would have to be crazy, right? That's what they're banking on. The defense will probably be 'not guilty by reason of temporary insanity.' "

"Maybe so. A person would have to be crazy to do what she did, the way she did it," Denton said.

"I believe she was crazy alright—crazy about Mr. Simmons. I've learned that Pearl wasn't the first woman he'd had a fling with. About six years ago, his wife found out about his affairs with some other women. She felt so dejected that she shot herself in the stomach. Now a woman would have to be pretty crazy about a guy to shoot herself instead of him.

"I believe Morgan told his wife, 'Look, honey, I don't love this woman, but she won't let me alone. She's threatened to testify against me if I stop seeing her and buying her things. You've got to help me out of this if I'm to stay out of jail and be with you and the kids.' "

"And he proposed murder, and she accepted," Denton said.

"Exactly."

"But will we be able to prove it?" Denton asked. "Mr. Simmons did, after all, accompany Miss Owens' body on the train back to Louisville. Doesn't that prove that he loved her, or at least had a strong sense of responsibility for what his wife had done?"

"I think it was all part of his plan. He wanted to stir up doubt. And look at these two news clippings from just after the murder." Sandusky handed the papers to Denton.

"Look at the places I've marked. You'll notice in the first paper he said he believed his wife would have shot him, too, if he hadn't run out of the car. In the next day's paper, he denied saying that. He said his wife would not have shot him. Looks to me as if he was afraid the first statement made her look a little too enraged. I believe the second version is the truth. Ina loves Morgan, and she committed murder to protect him. That was her motive."

"This is going to be quite a trial, isn't it?" Denton asked.

Sandusky could see that the young attorney was eager for the court date to arrive.

"It's shaping up that way," Sandusky said. "I want you to contact the witnesses on this list, starting with Miss Catherine Williams in Whitley City. She loaned Ina Simmons the dress and wide brim hat she was wearing on the train, as well as the hatbox that the police believe she was carrying the murder weapon in."

"According to the papers, neither Mr. Simmons nor Pearl recognized Mrs. Simmons in that outfit."

"I'm sure Pearl didn't recognize her, but I believe Mr. Simmons did. It wasn't important for him to know just where she was. The important thing was that Morgan and Pearl would be easy for Ina Simmons to find."

"So borrowing this disguise from Miss Williams will go toward proving that Mrs. Simmons wasn't temporarily insane. She planned the whole thing far in advance."

"That's how I'm hoping the jury will see it."

Sandusky checked off another line on his list. "That should keep you busy for a while," the elder attorney said.

"I'll get back to you as soon as I'm finished." Howard placed his notes into a briefcase and left the room.

Sandusky smiled as Denton walked out the door. He felt confident that the young attorney would do a good job. He liked Howard, and looked forward to prosecuting the case with him.

While Morgan continued to gather physicians as witnesses for Ina's case, attorney Boyd Morrow grew increasingly uneasy. Neither he nor attorney Cline had ever defended a woman against a murder charge, and since the murder appeared premeditated, the state would probably seek the death penalty for a guilty verdict. If they failed to successfully defend Ina, her two children would soon be motherless.

With that thought weighing upon him, Morrow told H. M. Cline he felt they should bring another attorney into the case, one well-versed in murder trials from both sides of the bench—former McCreary County judge R. L. Pope, who was now practicing law in Knoxville, Tennessee. Cline, whose practice had been confined primarily to his own small, rural region of Kentucky, agreed with the more worldly Morrow, who had, after all, been the legal advisor to his brother, Kentucky Governor Ed Morrow, from 1919-23.

Morrow phoned Pope, who was familiar with the highly-publicized case and welcomed the opportunity to join the defense team. Soon, the three men began meeting and corresponding regularly to plan their strategy.

On Tuesday, February 12, 1929, Ina, accompanied by a brother and sister, arrived in Somerset at the Newtonian Hotel, where she was reunited with her daughters. Ina had lived with her parents on their Junction City farm since her release on bond in August, and her daughters had remained in Whitley City with a former neighbor.

During those months, Ina and her children had not seen or communicated directly with Morgan, but attorney Cline had assured Morgan that his daughters were coping with his absence. Later that evening, Morgan would check into a room on the same floor of the four-story Newtonian Hotel.

While Ina, her daughters, and her sister, accompanied the luggage up to their rooms, Ina's father, Chris Cummings, was speaking to reporter Gerald Griffin in the lobby.

"How do you think the trial is going to go, Mr. Cummings?" Griffin asked.

"Ina's going to be found not guilty," Chris said. "We've got letters that'll show the kind of relations my daughter's low-down husband was having with that harlot. I don't think the jury will hold it again' Ina for trying to protect her family."

"But what if they do hold her accountable?" Griffin asked, playing the devil's advocate.

"We'll have to wait and see, won't we?" Cummings replied as he walked into the elevator.

Ina had packed enough clothing for five days for herself and her children; none of her attorneys could predict exactly how long the trial might take, but she felt five was a safe number. If the unthinkable happened and she was found guilty, perhaps, she reasoned, they would allow her to wear some of her own dresses in prison.

Ina's oldest daughter, Melissa, was with her in the room as she began unpacking. She was unaware her mother had packed so many clothes, and became alarmed.

"Momma," she asked, "are you going to be gone for a long time?" Tears welled in her eyes after she asked the question.

"No, darling," Ina embraced her daughter. "Momma isn't going anywhere. I just didn't know how long we would have to be in town. Look inside your bag, and you'll see I brought just as many outfits for you and your sister."

Melissa hurried from her mother's arms and popped open her own suitcase on the floor. "You're right, Momma." She smiled with relief. "It pays a body to be prepared, don't it?"

"It surely does," Ina said. She silently prayed she would be strong enough to face the worst, if the guilty verdict should come.

Later that evening, after Ina had put the children to bed, her father stopped by to offer words of encouragement.

"How's my girl doing?" he asked.

"Not good, Daddy. I feel like it's all over. I just know they're going to find me guilty and kill me. My babies are going to have to grow up without a mother." Ina started sobbing.

"Now, now, Ina." Chris put his arms around her. "Don't have so little faith. No jury's going to blame you for doing the right thing."

Ina backed out of her father's arms, but reached out to grasp his right hand.

"Daddy, I always did the right thing. Look what it's got me. I went to church every Sunday, cooked and cleaned for my family, loved my husband. But was that enough for Morgan? Hell no! He always had to run off to the city and take up with the tramps. He had to have the wild life. A country woman wasn't good enough for him."

"It wasn't that, Ina. Some men lose their heads when they meet up with them town women."

Ina released his hand, and her face grew flush.

"Are you making excuses for Morgan?"

"No. Not at all. I'm just saying the flesh is weak. Morgan's not the first man to give in, and I figure he won't be the last."

"Daddy, I'm not in the mood to hear about Morgan's weak flesh. I know you mean well, but I'd like to be alone." Ina rose on her tiptoes to kiss her father on the cheek. "Tell Momma I'm doing just fine, and that I love her and hope she gets to feeling better."

After Chris left the room, Ina turned out the light and got into bed. Before she finally went to sleep, she cursed Pearl, who, even in death, had continued to deny her and her children the right to live their lives in peace.

CHAPTER 9

By 7:30 on the morning of February 13, 1929, more than five hundred people had gathered outside the Somerset Courthouse. Scores of people waited against the front door and around the five columns of the front of the Greco-Roman structure. When the front doors opened at 8:00, the crowd surged up the stairs to the second floor courtroom of the circuit court.

The large, rectangular room sloped downward from the rear, towards the judge's bench. A waist-high banister, with a gate near each end, ran the width of the room, separating the audience from the jury and bench area. The backs of two elevated rows of six swivel chairs for the jury faced the audience. The court reporter sat at a small desk between the judge's bench and the jury. To the left of the judge's bench were the prosecution's tables; to the right were the tables for the defense.

Within moments, the five hundred available seats were filled. Then, at least two hundred more people crowded along the walls and in the aisles. Attorneys for the prosecution and the defense entered from the anteroom.

The bailiff requested that all rise for the honorable Judge Roscoe C. Tartar. The short, stout gentleman, whom some townsfolk thought resembled actor W. C. Fields, proudly took the bench. With one blow from his legendary gavel, court was called to order. According to newspaper accounts, the gavel had been carved from the wood of an oak tree that once stood over the grave of Confederate General Felix K. Zollicoffer, who was killed nearby at the battle of Mill Springs.

Tartar, a brilliant scholar who spent most of his life delving through literary classics in the library, had narrowly defeated incumbent Judge H. C. Kennedy in the preceding fall's elections.

This was the most sensational case he had presided over, and the most publicized trial in Pulaski County's history. Tartar had read all the initial newspaper accounts and kept up with the gossip about town for the past six months. He was aware that the majority of the county's citizens wanted to see Mrs. Simmons and her daughters walk right out of the courtroom and live happily ever after, but he had not been elected to do the will of the people.

A city woman, perhaps an immoral person to the countryfolk's way of thinking, had been murdered by a woman from these hills, but he had insisted to the press that justice would be done in his courtroom.

The first order of business was the selection of jurors. Thirty people were already in the courthouse awaiting their turn to take the jury box. One by one, the potential jurors were asked by prosecuting attorney J. S. Sandusky if they had formed or expressed an opinion as to the guilt or innocence of the defendant. He further asked if they had any objection to the application of the death penalty, in the event of a guilty verdict.

By the time the questioning had been completed, twenty-one of the potential jurors said they had already formed and expressed opinions on the case. Among them were seven women who stated they believed Ina was not guilty. They were summarily dismissed. Eight men on the panel stated that they had not formed an opinion and believed they could fairly try the case, but Judge Tartar dismissed each of them because he doubted their sincerity.

Ina's attorneys were outraged after the dismissal of each of these men, and registered their objections, but each objection was overruled.

"I believe," Judge Tartar said, "there has been far too much publicity and talk within the bounds of this town and this county for us to find even twelve unprejudiced jurors. I want to be fair to both sides. For that reason, I am hereby instructing Sheriff Jack W. Edwards to summon 100 potential jurors from our neighboring Wayne County in the hope that twelve of them will be suitable to pursue justice in this matter."

"Objection, your honor." Boyd Morrow jumped to his feet. "The state's attorney is a resident of Wayne County. Choosing a jury of his neighbors will give the prosecution an unfair advantage in these proceedings."

"Objection noted and overruled," Judge Tartar said.

"The defense will file an exception today in this matter, your honor," replied Morrow.

"That is within your rights as counsel for the accused," the judge said. "Court is now adjourned until 9 a.m. tomorrow morning, February 14, 1929."

Judge Tartar's gavel dropped, and the noisy crowd began exiting the courtroom. Prosecution and defense attorneys were approached by members of the press before they could leave the courtroom.

"Mr. Sandusky, do you consider today's actions a small victory for the state's case?" asked Elbert Raney of *The Louisville Times*.

"Not at all," the attorney replied.

46

"But all of the prospective jurors are from your home county of Wayne, sir," Raney said.

"I honestly don't think that will have any bearing on the outcome one way or the other," Sandusky answered. "Judge Tartar merely wants to draw upon jurors from a region that hasn't lived every day for the past six months with news and gossip about this case."

Local reporter Gerald Griffin, correspondent for *The Louisville Courier-Journal*, questioned defense attorney Boyd Morrow.

"How do you feel about Judge Tartar's decision to look outside the county for jurors?" Griffin asked.

"I'm outraged, and the people of Pulaski County will be also. The very idea that there are not twelve honest, unprejudiced citizens in this county is preposterous. There must be 5000 suitable jurors within the confines of Pulaski County."

"Last night, Mrs. Simmons' father told us that letters between Mr. Simmons and Miss Owens will be introduced as evidence of their relationship. Can you tell us anything about the content of these letters?"

Whitley City attorney H. M. Cline stepped forth to answer. "To the best of my knowledge, my client has never told me about the existence of any letters. If there were any letters, I believe I would know about them by now."

"What will be the defense's plea?" Griffin asked. "Rumor has it that you will enter a plea of emotional insanity and the unwritten law."

"Rumor has it correct this time," Morrow replied.

The unwritten law, or the right of the individual to kill in the heat of passion when the sanctity of the family was threatened by an outsider, was currently a popular defense across the nation in cases involving crimes of passion. Kentucky newspapers reporting on the murder of Pearl Decker Owens also included articles covering the trial of a teenager in Wyoming, charged with killing a rancher because he had been having an affair with the boy's mother. Attorneys for the youth had invoked the unwritten law as his defense.

"How will today's decision on the jurors affect your defense of Mrs. Simmons?" Griffin asked.

"It does appear to give an advantage to the prosecution. I'm further concerned that every day extra that this poor woman has to endure the emotional stress of this trial is an abomination. There's no reason on this earth that my client should have to endure this needless delay when fair jurors were right here in this courtroom today."

"What further action do you intend to take to protest Judge Tartar's decision?" Griffin asked.

"As you heard, we filed an exception to his action. We anticipate filing official papers later today. Now, if you'll excuse us, Mr. Griffin. Mr. Cline,

Mr. Pope, and I have an obligation to meet with our client."

Ina's defense counsel walked out of the courthouse and across the street to the Newtonian Hotel. The brief interview with the reporters had given Ina's father sufficient time to rush to his daughter's room and bring her up to date on the day's events. When the three defense attorneys walked into their client's room, they were verbally assaulted at the door.

"What have you got to say for yourselves, gentlemen?" Ina shouted nervously at them. "This is going to give Sandusky the jump on us, isn't it? He's going to have a jury made up of all his neighbors hanging on every word he says about me."

"Mrs. Simmons, I assure you that this is only a momentary setback," Boyd Morrow said as he attempted to place his hand on Ina's shoulder to calm her.

Ina backed out of his reach. "Mr. Cline," she scolded, "you had better get these men to doing what you said they would do. I'm not going to prison over this. I was justified in doing what I did on that train. Just ask anybody on the street out there. Ask any of them."

Ina's daughters were in the room, and began crying at their mother's outburst. Their grandfather stepped between their mother and her attorneys and said, "You'll have to forgive Ina. The strain is getting to be too much for her." He turned to Ina's sister and told her to take the children downstairs for ice cream.

After the children left, Boyd Morrow sat down on the bed next to Ina. "Mrs. Simmons," he said, "I want you to calm down. Take this pen in hand over at the desk and write out the words I'm going to dictate to you. This is an affidavit that we're going to file in the courthouse as an exception to Judge Tartar's decision to go out of the county for his jury."

"On the way over to the hotel, several leading citizens of this community expressed a desire that they would also like to file affidavits in your behalf," Cline added. "They share our belief that you can get a fair trial by a jury made up entirely of citizens of Pulaski County."

"What good is this going to do us?" Ina asked.

"Not much if we win, but it might be grounds for an appeal later if we lose," Morrow answered.

After Ina had transcribed the document, Morrow said to attorneys Cline and Pope, "A sweet idea just came to me. I know how we can equalize this Wayne Country jury, maybe even tip things a little in our direction."

"What do you have in mind?" Cline asked.

"Since it looks like the jury is going to be from Wayne County, and the state's attorney is from Wayne, it would appear the defense needs its own attorney from Wayne," Morrow said.

"I see where you're coming from," Cline said, with a grin that stretched from ear to ear. "H. C. Kennedy, right? Who better than the man Judge

Roscoe Tartar kicked out of the judge's bench in the election last fall? H. C. was the commonwealth attorney before he was elected to the judiciary. All that experience would be a big plus for our side if we can get him."

"Mr. Kennedy is well known and respected all the way to Tennessee," agreed attorney Pope.

"Now, Mr. Cummings, the question is, do you think you and your friends can afford one more attorney?" Morrow asked.

"Question is, can we 'ford not to?" Chris replied. "You'll get the money, if I have to sell the shirt off my back to get it for you. My daughter and my grandbabies mean everything to my missus and me."

With Ina's father's blessing, Morrow later phoned H. C. Kennedy.

"H.C., this is Boyd Morrow. I have a proposition for you."

"Ok, let's hear it," Kennedy replied.

"I assume you've heard about the Simmons' murder trial?"

"Yeah. My old buddy, Roscoe Tartar, is presiding over that one, isn't he?"

"That's right. He decided today that he couldn't find twelve unbiased jurors in Pulaski County, so he's sent the sheriff into your neck of the woods to round up some—"

"And seeing as I'm from Wayne, that might give you a leg up on the jury?"

"That," Morrow admitted, "and the hope that you'd like to visit your old courtroom again."

"From the other side of the bench," Kennedy laughed. "Count me in. I reckon old Roscoe will get a kick out of having me in his courtroom."

CHAPTER 10

Sheriff Jack W. Edwards had worked all day and into the evening rounding up jurors. Before returning to Somerset, he had enlisted 100 male citizens of Wayne County to come to Pulaski County bright and early the next morning. Judge Tartar had specified "100 persons," but the sheriff personally chose to interpret the order to be for 100 men.

The temperature was unusually mild for Valentine's Day. As reporters would note in the background for their stories that day from Somerset, birds were singing in the trees outside the courthouse, and a feeling of spring was in the air.

Just as on the day before, hundreds of men and a great many women from Somerset and the surrounding communities had abandoned their jobs and housekeeping for the opportunity to watch their legal system in action. Somerset had held murder trials in the past, but this one was a real novelty because the accused was a woman.

To most of the men and women in Somerset, Ina's victim was a "city woman," an appellation synonymous with "cigarette-smoking, whiskey-drinking man chaser." Liberated women such as Pearl straddled the line between acceptable male and female behavior, and therefore were perceived as a threat to both sexes. Many citizens felt justice had already been served on the train, and all that remained was the formality of the law granting its official approval with a not-guilty verdict.

The crowd was milling about the courthouse, waiting for the doors to the theater of justice to open and admit them. Peddlers along the street sold bag lunches and popcorn for those who planned to spend the entire day inside the courtroom. Of course, there would be a recess for lunch, but there was not much chance that a spectator could regain a seat once it was relinquished. A courtroom twice the size could not have held the previous day's crowd, and if anything, today's crowd was even larger.

Soon after the doors opened, all the seats were filled, along with every possible standing space in the aisles, along the walls, and in the front doorway and windowsills. The crowd grew silent when they saw Ina emerge from the anteroom with a daughter clinging under each arm, followed close behind by her attorneys. Ina's sister, Susan, and her three brothers, Albert, Joseph, and Clem, were seated at the defense table. State's attorney J. S. Sandusky, along with Howard Denton and newly-assigned county attorney G. W. Shadoan, were already seated at their table.

"We're with you all the way, Ina!" shouted someone in the crowd. The entire mob rose to its feet and began applauding and whistling in support of Ina. The accused woman, wearing a stylish dark blue suit coat and matching felt hat, looked frail, and as one reporter would state in his article, hardly looked like a cold blooded killer. Ina offered a slight smile to her hundreds of well-wishers, then took her seat.

The honorable Judge Roscoe Tartar was announced, and court was called to order. Before the business of the previous day could resume, attorney W. Boyd Morrow for the defense rose from his chair and said, "Your honor, before we continue the process of jury selection, the defense would like to make a motion for dismissal of the charges against Mrs. Simmons, on the grounds that there is a serious error on the indictment."

The attorney paused for an instant, and the only sound was the dull buzz of dozens of conversations triggered by the surprising announcement.

"And what is the nature of this serious error?" Judge Tartar asked.

"The front of the true bill has omitted the last two figures of the year that this crime was alleged to have occurred, your honor," Morrow said. "And on the inside of the bill, the date in August that this alleged crime occurred has been left blank."

"Your honor," Commonwealth Attorney J. S. Sandusky said, "the prosecution moves that the true bill be amended to reflect the date of the murder. There is nothing alleged about this crime, and the victim now rests in her eternal grave." Sandusky resumed his seat, visibly angered at the defense's technical ploy.

"It is so moved that the indictment be amended to reflect that the shooting occurred on the morning of August 10, 1928, if memory serves, which I'm certain in this instance that it does," Judge Tartar said.

"The defense would like it noted that we take exception to this ruling," Boyd Morrow said.

"So noted," Judge Tartar said. "Now, we will resume with the selection of the jury."

After each potential juror took the jury box, he was questioned by Sandusky as to whether he had formed an opinion regarding the case, and whether he objected to the death penalty in case of a guilty verdict. In addition to these questions, the Wayne County residents were also asked if they were acquainted with Mr. Morgan Simmons, and if they had seen him in Wayne County in recent days speaking with Dr. T. L. Hamlin, an announced witness for the defense.

Several of the potential jurors admitted they had seen Mr. Simmons speaking to Dr. Hamlin, but none knew anything about their conversation.

Attorney H. C. Kennedy, who had lost his seat on the bench to Judge Tartar in the previous autumn's elections, began his first day on the job by questioning potential jurors for the defense. When one man was dismissed by Judge Tartar because he had admitted to knowing Mr. Morgan Simmons, attorney Kennedy exploded.

"Your honor, the defense has the right to question this man about the level of his acquaintance with Mr. Simmons. For all we know, he merely meant that he knows who Mr. Simmons is when he sees him on the street."

"Overruled," Judge Tartar said. "Next, please."

Sandusky resumed his questioning. Several more potential venirmen admitted to prior knowledge of the case, and at each admission, Judge Tartar dismissed them before Kennedy could question for the defense. Each time, Kennedy angrily objected, and each time Tartar overruled.

In the opinion of many spectators, with each "overruled," Tartar was reminding Kennedy who had won the election. Kennedy had held the bench from 1923 to 1928. Now in his mid fifties, law had been his passion since childhood, and he showed no signs of slowing down after his defeat in the election.

Kennedy had received no formal legal education, but had studied the law books of attorneys in his hometown of Monticello in Wayne County. His preparation was sufficient to enable him to pass the bar, and a life-long career in law began.

Most of the 100 men from Wayne County were familiar with Kennedy, the second Republican ever to be elected County judge in Wayne County. After serving out his term, he had been elected circuit judge of the 28th Judicial District. During his term on the circuit court bench, the judge had gained a reputation as a bitter, relentless foe of the Ku Klux Klan, which had in excess of 1,000 members in Pulaski County alone. Many voters across the district believed that the political backlash from Kennedy's opposition to the Ku Klux Klan had cost him the fall election. Somerset's own Judge Tartar had received enough of the protest votes to win the contest and now sat on the bench.

Boyd Morrow was upset at what he perceived as Judge Tartar's cavalier treatment of the latest member of his team, but he remained composed at the defense table. If Judge Tartar's handling of Kennedy's objections seemed a tad unfair to the twelve Wayne County jurors who were eventually accepted, perhaps, Morrow thought, the defense would have already accomplished some of what it hoped to achieve by hiring Kennedy as co-counsel.

CHAPTER 11

By noon, the prosecution and the defense had agreed upon six of the required twelve jurors. Along the way, the Commonwealth had used 4 of its allotted 5 challenges, and the defense had used 6 of its 15 challenges. After three hours of combative selection, Judge Tartar adjourned for lunch.

Ina, accompanied by her daughters, father, sister, brothers, and four attorneys, exited the courthouse and walked to a restaurant across the public square. Ina's husband, Morgan, watched her as he sat at the base of one of the columns at the front of the Newtonian Hotel. Ina looked straight ahead and gave no indication that she had seen him.

The day before, Morgan had told a member of the press that he hoped his wife would be acquitted of the charges against her, but he denied he had spoken to her since the night of the shooting. Morgan, of course, had been in close contact with Cline, Ina's attorney in Whitley City, and he had done all that he could to help prepare his wife's case.

He had contacted all the physicians on the list Cline had given him. All of them were now in town, prepared to testify for the defense. If Ina received a guilty verdict, Morgan doubted that her father would ever let him see his daughters again. Morgan knew his family's future would soon lie in the hands of twelve men from Wayne County.

Court resumed just after 1 p.m. The courtroom was hot and smelled musty from the presence of the overflow crowd, most of whom had remained in their seats and partaken of bag lunches or skipped eating altogether. During the recess, the Somerset Undertaking Company had brought in paper fans, which were being put to good use on sweating faces and necks across the courtroom.

Within the next ninety minutes, the remaining six jurors were selected. The twelve men on the jury included: W. W. Burgess, blacksmith; Luther

Dobbs, farmer; John Dwyford, farmer; Otho Davidson, truck driver; Ellis Cooper, salesman; J. M. Burke, merchant; D. S. Stevens, farmer; Alonzo Morris, farmer; Gobel Jones, farmer; William Upchurch, farmer; Sam Blake, farmer; and E. M. Thompson, farmer.

"Is the prosecution prepared to make its opening statement?" Judge Tartar asked.

"Yes, we are, your honor," J. S. Sandusky said. The tall attorney eased from his chair and stood to face the jury. He picked up a copy of the indictment from his table and began to slowly read the words written on the document:

"The Grand Jury of Pulaski County, in the name and by the authority of the Commonwealth of Kentucky, accuse Ina Simmons of the crime offense of willful murder committed as follows: The said Ina Simmons in the County and Commonwealth aforesaid, on the tenth day of August 1928 and within twelve months before the finding of this indictment, did unlawfully, willfully, maliciously, feloniously and of her malice aforethought, kill, slay and murder Pearl Owens by shooting the said Pearl Owens, in and upon the head, body, arms, limbs and person with a pistol, a deadly weapon from which shooting and wounding the said Pearl Owens did then and there die."

Sandusky paused as if to allow time for his words to sink in. Then, in an emotionless tone, he added, "Gentlemen of the jury, we are seeking the death penalty for this crime." He turned, faced the judge's bench, and said, "I have nothing further, your honor."

The defense attorneys were visibly surprised by this brief opening, as were the hundreds of spectators behind the railing. Scores of discussions erupted in the audience, and the judge pounded his gavel and called for order.

When calm was restored, W. Boyd Morrow arose from his chair and adjusted the lines of his tailored suit. With his trademark gold-headed cane in hand, the distinguished attorney stood and sauntered up to the jury to begin the opening statement for the defense.

The audience grew silent in anticipation of his words. W. Boyd Morrow, known across Pulaski County as a scholarly attorney, had served as legal advisor to his brother, Kentucky Governor Edwin P. Morrow during his 1919 to 1923 term. While he didn't possess his brother's flare for spontaneous philosophizing, Boyd was known as a dynamic, incisive speaker in his own right.

In a calm, measured tone, Morrow began his opening statement to the jury, and the overflow crowd listened eagerly to every word.

"Today, gentlemen of the jury, the lives of Mrs. Ina Simmons, Miss Pearl Decker Owens, and Mr. Morgan Simmons will be bared in this courtroom. These three people were involved in a love triangle which ended in the death of Miss Owens.

"The state has charged the mother of the two children you see before you with the willful and malicious, premeditated murder of Miss Owens. The defense will admit that the evidence will show that Mrs. Simmons, a true and loving mother and wife, out of desperation took the life of Pearl Decker Owens, a 'scarlet woman' who relentlessly pursued Mrs. Simmons' husband."

"Objection, your honor," Sandusky said. "There has been no evidence introduced which reflects the deceased as a woman of ill repute."

"Sustained," Judge Tartar said.

"If," Morrow emphasized the word to express his own doubt, "Ina Simmons did slay Pearl Owens, her taking of that life was not willful, malicious, or premeditated."

Morrow continued, "Mrs. Ina Simmons, in an act of momentary insanity, and in the grip of primal emotion, fought to protect the home she had built for her two innocent babies with a husband and father who was, as you will see, undeserving of their love. Any other man would have thanked God Almighty for such a sweet, loving family, but Mr. Morgan Simmons was not satisfied.

"As Mrs. Simmons will tell you in her own words, her husband, from the early days of their marriage, sought out the carnal affections of other women on numerous occasions, causing her great emotional anguish and physical sickness.

"At the tender age of seventeen, Mrs. Simmons wed Morgan Simmons. Within one year, she had given him a daughter, the elder of the children you see here today. Mrs. Simmons invested all of her love and energies into making a happy home for her husband, and she thought that he was happy and everything was going well.

"Then, about six years ago, Mrs. Simmons learned that nothing was as it seemed. She discovered that her beloved husband, whom she had just blessed with their second precious child, had been seeking the bedroom affections of numerous other women.

"She was so devastated by his betrayal that she lost the will to live. Not even the love of her two babies could sustain her. In her desperation, Mrs. Ina Simmons placed a gun against her own body and pulled the trigger.

"Miraculously, Mrs. Simmons, after a long convalescence, recovered from her self-inflicted wound. Her straying husband returned in shame to her side and treated her with the loving kindness which she and their children deserved. At last, they seemed to be a happy family.

"Mr. Simmons, with the campaign support of his wife, was elected and served two terms as a clerk in the McCreary County Courthouse. She later encouraged him to run for the office of clerk of the circuit court of McCreary County, and again with her moral support, he won the election.

When he took office, she served side by side with him as his chief deputy, a position which required her to serve as clerk in his absence.

"Mrs. Simmons felt they had never been closer, but once again, things with Mr. Simmons were not as they seemed. Mr. Simmons' new position afforded him the opportunity to travel to Lexington in January of 1927 for a meeting of circuit court clerks from across the state. Apparently, it's here that Miss Pearl Decker Owens enters our story.

"Mr. Simmons began an affair with Miss Owens which remained a secret until Miss Owens called Mr. Simmons at work in the summer of 1927. Mrs. Simmons had answered the phone, but Pearl Owens insisted on speaking to Mr. Simmons. At this point, Mrs. Simmons became justifiably suspicious of her husband. Shortly thereafter, Mr. Simmons presented his wife with a suspicious telegram which ordered him to come to Lexington on urgent business.

"She secretly followed him on a later train, and asked for him at the door of his Lexington hotel room. A woman, who claimed to be the maid, answered the door and said Mr. Simmons was not in. As Mrs. Simmons was to learn later, that woman was, in fact, Pearl Decker Owens.

"Mrs. Simmons had not caught her husband in the act of being unfaithful, but she remained suspicious each time he left town unexpectedly. This nervous strain began to physically tell upon Mrs. Simmons, as physicians will testify for the defense. She began to lose weight and fell once more into depression.

"On Christmas Eve of 1927, the phone rang in her Whitley City home, and her suspicions were realized. Miss Pearl Owens was on the line, and this time she was glad to speak to Mrs. Simmons. She identified herself and said, 'Tell Morgan that I don't want to see him in Danville for Christmas because I'm mad at him.'

"Now, Mrs. Simmons knew that her terrible suspicions were true. This was the same woman who had called her husband at work—the woman her husband had been going all across Kentucky to meet for days at a time.

"Mr. Simmons, of course, denied having relations with Miss Owens. He said they were merely good friends and nothing more, but Mrs. Simmons knew better. Mr. Simmons refused to discuss the situation with his wife, and told her the whole matter was just her imagination. Her mental condition grew worse, and on the advice of her family physician, she was hospitalized in Lexington.

"As a witness for the defense will testify, Miss Pearl Owens had the audacity to stay overnight in Mrs. Simmons' home with Mr. Simmons and these two children while their mother was struggling for her sanity in that Lexington hospital."

The audience gasped. Once again, spectators started talking to each other, and the judge pounded his gavel for order.

With order restored, Morrow continued.

"A short period after Miss Owens had defiled the sanctity of her rival's home, the house burned. All of the family's belongings were destroyed.

"When Mrs. Simmons returned from the hospital, she and her family lived for several months in the Whitley City Hotel, before renting a house. The homeowners insurance was supposed to provide Mrs. Simmons with $600 to replace the clothing and furniture she had lost, but the money didn't come. She and her children continued to wear hand-me-down clothing, while her husband insisted that he had not seen a cent of the money."

Morrow walked to the opposite end of the jury, paused for a moment, tapped the tip of his cane on the top of his right shoe, and then continued.

"Once again, Mr. Simmons was called away on business. He said he was sorry his recovering wife could not accompany him on this trip; all the while he was planning to slip away to meet Miss Owens again at the same hotel.

Mrs. Simmons again followed her husband to Lexington—even though he had said he was going to Tennessee. Once in Lexington, Mrs. Simmons ran into the woman who had claimed to be a hotel maid some months prior. Mrs. Simmons confronted that woman, Pearl Decker Owens, who shamelessly admitted that she had been carrying on a relationship with Morgan Simmons. In her behalf, Miss Owens claimed that Simmons had told her that he had already separated from his wife and would soon be divorced.

"Miss Owens was dressed in fine furs and exquisite jewelry, which she said Mr. Simmons had purchased for her since they had been dating. Mrs. Simmons, standing there in a gingham dress that her mother had made, explained that she was surprised her husband could buy such expensive items when he only made one dollar per day working at the courthouse. As Pearl Owens spoke, Mrs. Simmons realized that this was where her insurance money had gone. This woman had received the compensation intended for her and her children for the loss of all their worldly possessions."

Several of the jurors shook their heads in dismay. Ina looked to the jury with tears rolling down her cheeks.

"Miss Owens noticed Mrs. Simmons' sudden change of demeanor, and promised that she would never see Mr. Simmons again, now that she knew he was still married. Mrs. Simmons told her husband of the meeting, and while he didn't confess to spending the insurance money on Miss Pearl Owens, he agreed never to see her again.

"Of course, as we know, Mr. Simmons had lied to his trusting wife once again. On the morning of August 9, 1928, Mr. Simmons presented Ina with another suspicious telegram, this one calling him to Somerset on business.

After he left town, Mrs. Simmons confronted the telegraph operator, who eventually admitted to writing the false message as Mr. Simmons dictated it. The operator was unaware, however, of Mr. Simmons' true destination.

"Mrs. Simmons decided to board the north-bound train near her home in hopes of catching her husband in his lie. In the past, when he had lied about his travels, he had usually headed to either Lexington or Louisville.

"Before she left home, Mrs. Simmons placed into a hatbox one of the many guns that her husband had lying around the house. This was not an unusual act for Mrs. Simmons. As a child of the hills, she was at ease with guns, and always carried one with her for protection any time she traveled alone on the train.

"She rode the train north to Danville. When the train pulled into the station, Mrs. Simmons saw Pearl Owens waiting to board. Miss Owens was alone, but Mrs. Simmons was suspicious and decided to remain on the train for its southbound route. Miss Owens apparently didn't notice Mrs. Simmons as she boarded the train. By this time, Mrs. Simmons went to sleep from sheer nervous exhaustion. She didn't awaken until after the train pulled out from the Somerset station.

"When she did awaken, she saw Miss Owens sitting with her arm around Morgan Simmons. That sight is the last thing Mrs. Simmons remembers before being taken into custody by Patrolman McKinley Matney and charged with the murder of Miss Owens."

Morrow paused briefly when he noticed Ina had started sobbing. In response to her mother's distress, Ina's youngest child started crying. Ina quickly regained her composure and held her daughter close to calm her.

The child stopped crying, and Morrow, pleased that the jurors had also noted the incident, continued.

"The defense will show, and as you will hear in Mrs. Simmons' own words, Pearl Decker Owens did everything in her power to win the affections of Morgan Simmons. She stalked this woman's husband like some kind of predatory beast, even after she had learned that her prey had lied to his poor wife. This Owens woman continually hunted the weak flesh of Morgan Simmons, which caused Mrs. Simmons unendurable anguish and sickness. In an instant of momentary insanity, Mrs. Ina Simmons was seized by a primal passion which unleashed its fury upon Pearl Owens.

"Mrs. Simmons' most basic instinct was to protect the sanctity of her family, her two little children and the undeserving husband who poorly provided for them. Mrs. Simmons killed to save her mate and protect her young from a cunning, relentless woman who threatened to tear their family apart.

"Gentlemen of the jury, I'm certain when you have heard all the details of this sorry story, you will agree that Mrs. Ina Simmons had the right to kill to save her family." Morrow raised his hand like a preacher testifying before God and said, "This right to kill for home and family is not written in the statute books of any law library across our land, but it is as basic as our God-given right to pursue happiness and to take up arms when our right to pursue that happiness is denied.

"In this country, as we are all aware, there is a separation of church and state. In this courtroom, we are bound by the laws of the state. It is the Commonwealth of the State of Kentucky which has asked for the life of the mother of these two children in exchange for the life of the woman who tried to deny them, and their mother, of their father.

"We cannot ask that you find her not guilty by virtue of an unwritten law, believe in it though we may. For this reason, by the laws of the state, we must ask that you weigh the evidence, then render a verdict of not guilty by reason of temporary insanity, which the law books do acknowledge and duly allow."

Morrow paused, and then walked slowly in front of the jury, establishing eye contact with each juror. At the end of the row, he stopped, planted his cane between his feet, and leaned, one hand upon the other, against the lion's head pommel.

"Gentlemen of the jury, when you have heard all the evidence in this case, you will really be given only two choices, and it will be as simple as this: you must vote for the death penalty and send this woman to the electric chair and her poor children to their wretched father, or you must find Mrs. Simmons not guilty, and thus allow her to continue to mother these two innocent children. Listen carefully and judge well, gentlemen, for their lives are in your able hands."

Across the audience, spectators sobbed and wiped their eyes.

W. Boyd Morrow turned from the jury and returned to his table.

Judge Tartar said, "Gentlemen of the jury, you have heard the opening statements of the prosecution and the defense. The state will now call its first witness."

Commonwealth attorney J. S. Sandusky rose from his chair and said, "State calls John Heinz to the witness stand."

A tall young man in a black suit approached the bench. After the witness was sworn in and seated, Sandusky asked, "What is your occupation, Mr. Heinz?"

"I'm a flagman for the Southern Railway."

"And where were you at midnight and the early morning hours of August 10, 1928?"

"I was on duty on the southbound train, in the rear of one of the passenger cars. The train pulled out of Somerset a few minutes before midnight."

"I understand that something unusual happened that night. Could you give us the details of what transpired in that car shortly after midnight?"

"Like I said, I was in the rear of the coach. I was looking toward the front, fixing to turn around and walk out the back door into the next car when I seen a woman jump up out of her seat on the right side of the car and walk into the center aisle."

"Do you see that woman here in the courtroom today?"

"Yes, that's her right over yonder." Heinz pointed toward Ina Simmons, seated at the defense table.

"Let the jury note that the witness has indicated Mrs. Ina Simmons," Sandusky said. "Did you continue to observe the woman?"

"No, I didn't think nothing of it, her jumping up that way. I just figured she knowed somebody and wanted to go up and talk. I turned around and started on out of the car. That's when I heared two loud bangs. When I turned back around, people was screaming and hunkering down under their seats. I figured somebody must be shooting right there in the car."

"Did you see Mrs. Simmons when you turned back around?"

"Yeah, she was the only one standing, except for a man who ran past her and bumped into me as I was coming up the car. Soon as I seen Mrs. Simmons, she kind of fell back down into a seat on the right side of the car. As I walked up the aisle, I seen a woman leaned over in her chair on the left side, directly 'cross from Mrs. Simmons. They was blood all over the back of her head and down the right side of her back."

"How would you describe her condition?"

"She looked dead to me. She wouldn't moving or making a sound or nothing."

"Did you look over at Mrs. Simmons after you saw the blood-covered woman?"

"Yeah. I went up to Mrs. Simmons, and a 38 pistol was laying on the seat beside her."

"Was this the gun you saw?" Sandusky held up a revolver with an identification tag tied around the trigger.

"Looks like it, or one just like it."

"Let the jury note that Mr. Heinz has identified exhibit number one," Sandusky said. "What happened to the gun?"

"The conductor, Dan Dean, picked it up. I think he give it to somebody at the roundhouse when he went to call the police."

"How did Mrs. Simmons appear to you?"

"She was going on something terrible, crying and shaking all over."

"Was she saying anything?"

"No, not that I recollect,"

"Thank you, Mr. Heinz. I have no further questions for this witness, your honor," Sandusky said.

"Defense's witness," Judge Tartar said.

"We have no questions at this time for the witness, your honor," defense counsel H. C. Kennedy said.

The state called its next witness, Dan Dean.

"What is your occupation, Mr. Dean?" Sandusky asked the middle-aged man.

"I'm a conductor for the Southern Railway."

"Were you in the same passenger car with Mr. John Heinz during the early morning of August 10, 1928?"

"Yes, I was."

"Did you hear any loud sounds?"

"Yes. I was in the front of the car collecting tickets when I heard what sounded like two gunshots. The people in the rear of the car were jumping for cover and screaming when I looked up. I immediately pulled the cord to stop the train at that point."

"What did you do next?"

"The train started slowing down; I looked back where the commotion had started. There hadn't been any more gunshots, so I walked back to John. He was looking at the woman who'd been shot. Mrs. Simmons over there," Dean pointed to Ina at the defense table, "was screaming in the seat across the aisle. I looked down in the seat beside her and saw a gun."

"The jury will note that Dan Dean has identified Mrs. Ina Simmons in the courtroom. Was this the gun you found?" Sandusky held up the pistol.

"Yes."

"Let the jury note that Dan Dean has also identified exhibit no. 1," Sandusky said. "Did you touch the weapon?"

"Yes. I picked it up and put it in my coat pocket. A little later, I gave the gun to A. C. Snyder at the roundhouse and asked him to call the police."

"What did you do immediately after putting the gun in your coat pocket?"

"I tried to calm the passengers down while John was trying to find something to cover up the dead woman."

"Did Mrs. Simmons have any luggage on board with her?"

"Nothing but a hatbox that was in the floor in front of the seat next to her."

"Is this the hatbox?" Sandusky picked the item up from the evidence table.

"It looks like it. Let me see it."

Sandusky handed Dean the box, and he read two tags tied to the handle.

"Yes, this is the hatbox. I remember it had two different people's names on it. One tag has the name and address of a Catherine Williams, and the other one has Mrs. Ina Simmons' name and address."

Dean returned the hatbox to Sandusky, and he placed it back on the evidence table.

"The jury will note that Mr. Dean has identified exhibit number two," Sandusky said. "Did you open the hatbox that night on the train, Mr. Dean?"

"No. I didn't have to. It was already lying open on the floor. I believe John Heinz gave it to the patrolman, McKinley Matney, when he came on board."

"I have no further questions, your honor," Sandusky said.

"The defense has no questions for the witness," Kennedy said.

Dan Dean was excused, and the state called roundhouse foreman A. C. Snyder to the stand. Snyder also identified the gun, and confirmed that he had called the police. He indicated that he had turned the pistol over to Somerset Police patrolman McKinley Matney when the officer came to the shop to retrieve the weapon. Again, the defense counsel had no questions for the state's witness, and A. C. Snyder was excused.

The state's next witness was Somerset patrolman McKinley Matney. The husky young man, who had worked as a logger just before joining the Somerset police force, removed his hat before placing his hand on the Bible to be sworn in.

"Mr. Matney, did you receive a call from A. C. Snyder on the early morning of August 10, 1928?" Sandusky asked.

"Yes, the call come into the office a little after midnight. I was at the site by 12:30 a.m."

"Could you describe the scene you found at Ferguson?"

"Most of the passengers was standing outside the train, around the steps of the day coach where the shooting had took place. Inside the car, John Heinz, the flagman, was waiting with Mrs. Ina Simmons."

"What was Mrs. Simmons' condition?"

"She seemed to be having a nervous breakdown. Kept asking for her babies and her husband, and she wouldn't able to answer any of the questions I put to her."

"Was her husband in the car?"

"No. He was outside with the rest of the crowd. I questioned him after I'd placed Mrs. Simmons under arrest and turned her over to Police Chief Warren."

"What did Mr. Simmons tell you?"

"He said he'd got on the train at Somerset, where he'd spent the day on business. Miss Owens, who he said he was slightly acquainted with, offered him a seat next to her on the train. They was talking when the train left the station, and the next thing he knowed, he heard the gunshots and seen Miss Owens fall forward. When he turned around, he seen his wife behind him with a gun in her hand, so he hightailed it out the back of the car."

"Objection!" Kennedy was on his feet. "This is hearsay. Morgan Simmons' statement to the patrolman cannot be entered into evidence because Mr. Simmons cannot be questioned or cross-examined in this courtroom."

"Sustained," Judge Tartar said.

"Did Mr. Simmons know his wife was on the train?" Sandusky asked.

"No. He said he wouldn't a recognized her in the outfit she was wearing, even if he had expected her to be on board."

"Did Mr. Simmons say he had planned to meet Pearl Owens?"

"No. He said he had no idea she would be onboard."

"Did Mr. Simmons say anything about why his wife would have reason to harm Miss Owens?"

"Yes. He said she had a crazy notion that Miss Owens had been seeing him, and that she'd been jealous over their friendship. Mr. Simmons said him and Miss Owens had never been anything more than friends."

"What was Mrs. Owens' condition when you arrived on the scene?"

"She was already dead. Somebody had placed a sheet over her, and blood had soaked through it. They was a lot of blood on the floor at her feet."

"Did you examine her wounds?"

"Yeah. They was two holes where bullets went in, and one hole where one went out. One bullet hit her in the back of her skull, and come out her temple about two inches over the left ear. The second bullet hit her right shoulder, where it probably lodged."

Sandusky turned to look at Ina Simmons before asking his next question. She looked detached, totally disinterested in the gory details of her crime.

"Were these wounds consistent with the size you would expect to be inflicted with a 38 caliber shell?"

"In my experience, I would say they was."

"Did you take possession of a hatbox belonging to Mrs. Simmons when you arrested her?"

"I did."

"Is this the hatbox?" Sandusky handed it to the patrolman.

"That's it."

"Let the jury note that the witness has identified exhibit number two. Did you open the box while you were on the train?"

"No. It was already open on the floor when I got there."

"What were the contents?"

"They was nothing inside."

"Did you find that odd?"

"Yeah, I did. Usually women don't carry a hatbox unless they have a extra hat."

"Did you see another hat lying about? Could she have dropped an extra hat onto the floor?"

"I didn't see nothing else on the scene, and I made a thorough search."

"If she wasn't carrying an extra hat, why do you think she had the hatbox?"

"Probably to carry the gun that was found beside her. Mrs. Simmons' dress was a clingy type of material, so there was no place on her person where she could have hid the pistol."

"Objection, your honor." H. C. Kennedy jumped to his feet. "Again, this is mere speculation on the witness' part. My co-counsel, Mr. Morrow, has admitted that Mrs. Simmons placed a gun in the hatbox, but just for the sake of argument, we must assume that there is no way Mr. Matney could know what Mrs. Simmons was going to do with that hatbox once she got where she was going. Maybe she was going to put the borrowed hat back into it later."

Judge Tartar sustained.

"Why, thank you, your honor," Kennedy said, eliciting much laughter from the audience as he sat back down. This was the first time Tartar had sustained one of Kennedy's more substantial objections.

"Couldn't she have carried the pistol in her purse?" Sandusky continued.

"If she had been carrying one. I never found a purse, and I'd made a point to look for one."

"Did you retrieve the gun on the train?"

"No. The conductor or the flagman, I forget which, had already give it to somebody at the Ferguson roundhouse. A. C. Snyder turned the gun over to me shortly after Chief Warren left with Mrs. Simmons."

"Is this the weapon you were given?"

Sandusky handed a 38 caliber revolver to the patrolman, and he briefly examined it.

"Yeah, yeah, this is the gun."

"The jury will note that the witness has identified exhibit number one," Sandusky said. "What did you find when you first examined the weapon?"

"They was three loaded and two empty cartridges in the gun."

"And how many times did you say Miss Owens had been shot?" Sandusky turned to look at the jury as he awaited Matney's reply.

"Two times."

"I have no further questions, your honor," Sandusky said.

"Defense's witness," Judge Tartar said.

Again, the defense had no questions for the witness. The next state witness called was O. W. Swain of the Somerset Undertaking Company.

"Mr. Swain," Sandusky asked, "were you called upon to embalm someone in your undertaking establishment during the early morning hours of August 10, 1928?"

"Yes, I received a call from the police that someone had been killed. Just after the body arrived, a Mr. Morgan Simmons came in. He said the deceased was a friend of his. Since the friend was from Louisville, he had called her family there to ask what they wished to be done with the body. They asked Mr. Simmons to make arrangements locally for preparing the body to be shipped to Louisville on the train."

"Could you describe the person who was brought to your establishment for embalming?"

"She was a white woman, approximately thirty years of age. She had short, dark hair, and was wearing a light blue dress. A very pretty woman."

"Upon examining her body, what did you determine as the probable cause of death?"

"Mr. Simmons told me she had been shot. That's what I found. There was a bullet hole in the back of her head, and another hole just about two inches over her left ear where the bullet came out. There was another hole in her right shoulder, but no exit wound. That one must have stayed inside her."

Again, Sandusky looked to Ina for a reaction. She seemed oblivious to the testimony as she nonchalantly combed her fingers through her youngest daughter's hair while the child drew a picture on a sheet from a legal pad.

"Did you attempt to remove the bullet from the shoulder?" Sandusky asked.

"No. I didn't see much use in it. Sometimes you have to cut around a lot just to find out where the bullet has gone if it's struck a bone."

"Did anyone else examine the wounds?"

"Yes. Police Chief Warren sent Dr. Norfleet over later that morning to make an official examination. That's the usual procedure in cases involving murder."

"Did you fill out the death certificate on the victim?"

"Yes."

"Who supplied you with the victim's name, address, age, etc?"

"Mr. Simmons gave me all of that information. He said he had known the woman for nearly two years, and seemed to know quite a bit about her."

"Did Miss Owens have any identification or personal effects upon her person?"

"No identification, but she was wearing several articles of jewelry. I have a list here with me . . . there were two diamond rings, a set ring, a pearl necklace, and a belt buckle."

"What was done with these personal effects?"

"I turned the rings over to Mr. Simmons in the embalming room. After I handed them to him, he asked if he could be alone with the body to remove the necklace himself. I told him I didn't see any harm in it."

"Did Mr. Simmons tell you what he was going to do with the jewelry?"

"He said he was going to turn it over to the woman's relatives. I assume that's what he did. All of the valuables had been removed when I returned to embalm the body."

"How would you describe Mr. Simmons' demeanor when you saw him? Was he sad, or grief stricken? Unconcerned? Unemotional?"

"I would say he seemed tired. Troubled, and concerned. He was concerned about complying with the family's wishes and getting the woman's body ready for the evening train."

"Mr. Swain, did your undertaking establishment put the body in the parlor for the public to view?"

"Yes, we placed her in the parlor, and hundreds of people came by all during the day for a look at her."

"Did you consider this an appropriate thing to do? After all, the woman wasn't from this area."

"My partner, Mr. Day, and I didn't think it would do any harm. There were a few people in town who knew her. They said she'd visited Somerset about two months before. You know how it is when something bad happens," Swain was defensive. "People always want to come in and have a look."

"Yes, unfortunately, Mr. Swain, I do know how people are. Your honor, I have no further questions for this witness."

The defense had no questions for Mr. Swain. The witness was excused, and the state called Somerset physician Carl Norfleet to the stand.

"Dr. Norfleet, did you examine the body of Miss Pearl Decker Owens in the Somerset Undertaking Company on the morning of August 10, 1928?"

"Yes, I did. Police Chief Warren called me about seven that morning and asked me to examine the body for an official determination of the cause of death."

"What were your conclusions?"

"I believe the woman died instantly from a bullet wound to the back of the head. The bullet probably passed through the brain before it exited her left temple over the ear."

"Were there any other wounds?"

"Yes. One in her right shoulder, an entrance wound. That one alone wouldn't have killed her, but the one in the head did without question."

"Your honor, we have no further questions for this witness," Sandusky said.

The defense declined to question Dr. Norfleet, and he was excused.

"The state calls Miss Catherine Williams," Sandusky said.

A fashionably-dressed, petite twenty-five-year-old woman took the stand and was sworn in.

"Miss Williams, do you know Mrs. Ina Simmons?"

"Yes. She moved into a rental house next door to me last summer."

"Did you see her anytime on August 9, 1928?"

"Yes. She came by early that morning. She had to make a trip to

Somerset and needed some decent clothing. All of her things had burned up in a house fire, and she said she was ashamed to wear her homemade dresses in public. She asked to borrow a black dress and its matching wide brim hat that she had seen me wear to church one Sunday."

"Did she borrow anything else?"

"Yes. She asked for a hatbox because hers had burned in the fire that destroyed her house."

"Had she ever borrowed any of your clothing before?"

"No. That was the first time."

"Did she say what she would be doing in Somerset?"

"No, she didn't say, and I didn't think it was any of my business to ask."

"Did you happen to see her leave her house later that morning?"

"Yes, she left in a taxi heading south. I thought that was kind of odd, because she needed to head north to get to Somerset."

"The state has no further questions for this witness, your honor."

"Defense's witness," Judge Tartar said.

To everyone's surprise, H. C. Kennedy, counsel for the defense, finally got up from the table and approached the witness stand.

"Mrs. Williams, did you think it was unusual that Miss Owens asked to borrow an outfit and a hatbox from you?" Kennedy asked.

"Heck, no, I would have done the same thing if all my clothes had been burned. A woman's got to keep up her image when she goes out in public. Mrs. Simmons' gingham dresses weren't sloppy or anything, but they weren't in fashion, either."

"You testified that you watched Mrs. Simmons after she left your house?"

"Yes. I saw her get into a taxi that headed south."

"But you don't know if she had to make a stop on the south side of town before heading to Somerset?"

"That is correct."

"Your honor, the defense has no further questions for this witness."

"In that case, the witness is excused," Judge Tartar said. "It's now 6 p.m. Court will adjourn until 7:30 this evening."

CHAPTER 12

Ina, her family, and the attorneys for the prosecution and the defense left the courthouse to take their supper in restaurants around the public square. Most of the spectators, however, remained in the chairs they had occupied for the past ten hours, too afraid of losing their seats to leave for a bite to eat. Rumors spread through the crowd that the case would continue long into the night, and that the jury might enter into deliberations before dawn.

In a private booth in the corner of a restaurant across the street from the courthouse, the state's three attorneys discussed over supper their plans for the balance of the evening.

"How do you think it's going, Schuyler?" county attorney G. W. Shadoan asked Sandusky.

"We've built a solid case. I think we've shown without question that Mrs. Simmons came on that train prepared to shoot Pearl Owens. She did shoot her, and the two missing bullets from the gun were the ones she fired at Pearl.

"I only wish we could try Morgan Simmons for his role in this assassination, but there's no evidence to show that he planned this whole thing. He had to tell his wife that Pearl would board the train in Danville. According to Boyd Morrow, it was a coincidence that Ina Simmons happened to see Pearl waiting to board a southbound train in Danville, but I'll never believe that. Even if it was a coincidence, why did Ina follow Pearl south, unless she knew she was going to meet Morgan in Somerset?"

"And she had already been told by the telegraph operator that the Somerset destination was a ruse, so Somerset was an unlikely meeting place," Howard Denton said.

"The more I think about this alleged telegram, the less I believe in its existence," Sandusky said.

"Did you get the telegraph operator to confirm Ina's story about the faked message?" Shadoan asked.

"I spoke with the woman who had been on duty, and of course, she denied knowledge of the whole thing," Denton replied. "There's not a chance she'd admit to it, anyway. She'd lose her job if she admitted to forging messages."

"It doesn't matter," Sandusky said. "It's convenient for Morgan Simmons either way. The jury will believe he paid off a telegraph operator to falsify a message so he could sneak around on his wife. Even without the operator's testimony, the jury will believe he did it.

"As I've told Howard, I believe Mr. Simmons cooked up this telegram story with his wife as part of the murder plot. I say Mrs. Simmons knew her husband would get on that train in Somerset, and that Pearl had told Morgan Simmons that she would meet him when the train stopped in Somerset. Morgan knew Pearl would be changing trains in Danville. He wanted his wife to position herself close by, so she could be 'driven insane with rage' when she caught the two of them together. I believe he probably put the gun in her hand when he walked down the aisle toward Pearl. The whole thing's too neat to fit together any other way."

"And according to Mrs. Simmons, most of her husband's meetings with Pearl occurred in Louisville or Lexington," Shadoan said. "As Boyd Morrow paints Pearl, she was not the kind of woman who could find enough excitement in a small town like Danville or Somerset."

"How do we get Mrs. Simmons to admit she knew Pearl would be waiting in Danville?" Denton asked. "Unless I forgot to check somebody off, we've already questioned all of our witnesses."

"That's just it," Sandusky said. "Unless someone else called Mrs. Simmons and told her that Pearl would be in Danville, Morgan Simmons has to be the one who told her. We can't put Morgan on the stand, and it's unlikely that 'someone else' is going to magically come forth. That means we're going to have to make Mrs. Simmons spill the truth."

"How do we do that?" Denton asked.

"By making her sweat it a little," Sandusky said. "After we recall some of our witnesses tonight, I'm going to ask for a continuance until tomorrow, to allow us time to bring in some new, surprise witnesses."

"And if somebody other than her husband told Mrs. Simmons about Danville, she will have to worry that they are going to talk?" Shadoan said.

"Yes," Sandusky said. "If Ina told someone else of her plans to murder Pearl, she's going to think they're ready to come forth with the information and help us establish premeditation. If there is a third party, I figure Ina will crack in the night and confess—if we offer to drop the death penalty in exchange for a life sentence."

"Sounds good," Denton said. "Now what's this about recalling some of our witnesses?"

"We want to put the jury to bed tonight thinking about the way in which Pearl was murdered, and about how her killer borrowed a disguise from her neighbor," Sandusky said. "All day long, those jurymen have had Ina's poor little children to look at. I want them to go to bed with visions of murder dancing in their heads. And if that doesn't work, at the very least we'll have a refreshed jury tomorrow."

Sandusky stopped to finish his coffee. He touched a napkin to the corners of his mouth, and then continued.

"I know most of those farmers on the jury. They've been up since long before dawn, and by the time we finish tonight, it'll be way past their bedtime. If they have to listen to the defense carry on for hours this evening, those men will agree she's not guilty just to get the whole thing over with."

When court resumed at 7:30, Sandusky followed through with his suppertime plan. Former state witnesses A. C. Snyder, undertaker O. W. Swain, and Catherine Williams were called in succession. With few exceptions, the state asked each witness essentially the same questions they had presented earlier, and received the same responses.

This time, when Sandusky questioned A. C. Snyder, he brought the gun close to the jury box so that each juror could get a good look at the instrument of Pearl Decker Owens' death. When he questioned undertaker Swain, he asked about the size of the entry and exit wounds, taking special care to emphasize that Pearl had been shot from behind. The defense declined to cross-examine Swain, but Kennedy did take the opportunity to question Snyder.

"Mr. Snyder, you testified earlier today that you gave the gun found on the train to patrolman Matney," Kennedy said.

"Yes."

"Do you remember who gave the gun to you that night?"

"It was either the conductor, Dean, or the flagman, Heinz. I seen a lot of both of them that night, but I don't recall exactly which one of them gave me the gun."

"But you are certain that you did give this gun to patrolman Matney when he came to the roundhouse?"

"No doubt about that. That's the gun."

"Did patrolman Matney examine the gun after you gave it to him?"

"No. I think he just walked out of the shop after he got it."

"Thank you. The defense has no further questions for this witness."

Judge Tartar excused Snyder, and Sandusky recalled Catherine Williams, whom he had been saving for last. In a new line of questioning, he asked her if Mrs. Simmons had asked to borrow more than one outfit, or any other articles of clothing, such as undergarments, shoes, or purses.

"I offered several outfits to her, but she said the one would be enough," Williams said.

"Allow me, if you will, Miss Williams, to ask a question of a personal nature. If you were traveling on a hot summer's day, such as August 9 of last year, would you wear an outfit like the one you loaned to Mrs. Simmons for more than one day before washing it?"

"I should say not, and I hope that Mrs. Simmons wouldn't either. Two days in a row on a hot, muggy train could have ruined the outfit."

"Do you believe she would have worn your dress two days straight?"

"No, I believe she would have respected anything I loaned her. She knew it was an expensive item."

"And she borrowed—"

"Your honor," Kennedy said, "I fail to see the significance of all this clothing talk? Does Mr. Sandusky have a point?"

"Mr. Sandusky?" Judge Tartar asked.

"Your honor," Sandusky replied, "in his opening statement, Mr. Morrow stated that Mr. Simmons and Pearl Owens usually met in Lexington or Louisville. I'm merely trying to establish that Mrs. Simmons apparently did not suspect her husband had sneaked away to either of those cities on the day he allegedly had a telegram falsified. The number of outfits Mrs. Simmons did or did not borrow may have a direct bearing upon how Mrs. Simmons came to encounter Pearl Owens in the Danville station."

"I'll allow you to continue with this line of questioning," Judge Tartar said.

"Thank you, your honor," Sandusky said. "Now, Miss Williams, do you believe Mrs. Simmons borrowed your outfit because she could not afford such an outfit of her own?"

"That's what I assumed. They had others just like it downtown—if she'd been able to buy one."

"In your opinion, then, since Mrs. Simmons borrowed only one outfit, and she was wearing that outfit on the train—and apparently had no money to buy a comparable one on her journey—does it appear to you that Mrs. Simmons intended to be away for just one day—say long enough to go to Danville and back?"

"That's the way it would appear to me."

"And if she had planned to travel to Louisville or Lexington, she probably would have carried a change of clothing?"

"I know I certainly would have."

"I believe Mrs. Simmons would have, also," Sandusky said. "Your honor, I have no further questions for this witness."

"Defense's witness," Judge Tartar said.

"Did Mrs. Simmons indicate to you that she had seen the dress in the downtown store?" Kennedy asked.

"No, she didn't."

"And did you tell her they were still for sale downtown?"

"No, I didn't. I thought that would sound like I didn't want her to borrow mine."

"So it's entirely possible that Mrs. Simmons borrowed your dress because she thought it was unique, or she didn't have time to shop for a new dress?"

"That's possible."

"Thank you, Miss Williams. No further questions, your honor," Kennedy said.

After the witness stepped down, J. S. Sandusky faced Judge Tartar and said, "Your honor, the state requests a continuance in these proceedings until tomorrow morning. We have several new witnesses who have come forth to testify, but they'll be unable to appear until tomorrow."

"The court grants your request. Court is adjourned until 9 a.m. tomorrow."

The audience, as well as the defense counsel, was stunned by this unexpected turn of events. While the hundreds of spectators began speculating with their neighbors about these surprise witnesses, defense counsel R. L. Pope sprang to his feet and ran to the front of the judge's bench.

"Objection, your honor," Pope said. "The defense is entitled to know the names of these witnesses."

"The Commonwealth has not previously asked for a list of any defense witnesses, your honor," Sandusky said. "It would be unfair to treat the defense differently after the trial has already gotten underway."

"Order in the court." Judge Tartar pounded his gavel.

Boyd Morrow ignored the judge's request and joined Pope in front of the judge's bench. "Your honor, the defense has a right to demand the names of all Commonwealth witnesses in order that the defendant can call rebuttal witnesses," Morrow said.

"Overruled," Judge Tartar said. "I represent the Commonwealth and the defendant, and I'm going to see that both sides get a fair trial. The court does not intend to be intimidated by counsel for either side."

The judge paused for a moment. He looked toward the defense table, and then to the prosecution.

"Gentlemen," he continued, "why the precipitate haste in this case? We will take our time and see that justice is done. Court is adjourned until 9 a.m." With a drop of his gavel, Judge Tartar ended the first day of the trial.

The judge stepped down from his bench and exited via the anteroom, followed close behind by the three attorneys for the state. A string of policemen separated Ina Simmons and her entourage from the crowd of well-wishers and accompanied them across the public square to the doors of the Newtonian Hotel.

CHAPTER 13

For most of the day, Morgan Simmons had waited on the front porch of the Newtonian, and occasionally, someone who had stood listening outside the courtroom doors would bring him an update on the trial. Since the trial had begun, Morgan had felt helpless, unable to influence events which he had set into motion.

He regretted that he had not divorced Ina and married Pearl. Pearl had pleaded with him to leave his wife, and promised him that she would give him ample time to visit with his children, but he had insisted on remaining in both worlds.

Life had been so intense, so thrilling with Pearl on their secret weekends, but from the start he had wondered how much of the delight was due to the forbidden nature of their relationship. After the first few weeks of their affair, he began to view his leisure time with Pearl as a reward for the boring hours he spent on the job and at home with Ina.

Morgan had been a hard-working man all of his life, and had never been able to enjoy any pleasure which he had not earned. Without the pain he allowed his marriage to inflict upon him, he wondered how long Pearl, or any woman, could have continued to intrigue him. All pleasure must have its price, Morgan reasoned, but Pearl should not have been the one to pay.

Morgan walked around Somerset for hours that night, trying to exhaust himself sufficiently that his body would demand a long, restful sleep. Shortly after midnight, he felt tired enough to retire. He returned to his room on the fourth floor of the Newtonian Hotel and went to bed.

After two nights with little sleep, Morgan expected to fall asleep quickly, but for at least an hour, he lay flat on his back with his eyes closed, thinking of Pearl. When sleep finally claimed him, he dreamed he was with her again . . .

Morgan and Pearl were sleeping after a wonderful, passionate evening.

They were in his house in Whitley City, resting in the bed that he had shared with his wife for the past ten years. Ina was away in a Lexington hospital. She had driven herself sick from worry over Morgan's relationship with Pearl, and her doctor had told him she would be hospitalized for at least a week.

Pearl, after receiving Morgan's call, arrived in Whitley City on the second day of her rival's hospitalization. Morgan introduced the beautiful, dark-haired woman to his children as a friend of their mother's, who had agreed to stay and care for them while their mother was away. The children had innocently welcomed Pearl. They told her she was pretty and admired her fine jewelry and clothing.

That evening, after Pearl told the children a bedtime story, she and Morgan retired to his bedroom. Perhaps because she was in Ina's bed, Pearl was more passionate that first night than she had ever been with Morgan. They made love like two wild beasts, then, exhausted, fell quickly into a deep sleep.

Up to this point, Morgan's dream was filled with events as they had actually happened, just weeks before his home was destroyed by a fire. Then, the events of his dream took on their own reality. Morgan now dreamed that he awoke in the middle of the night and turned to look at his beloved Pearl. The bed was next to the window, and there was just enough light from the full moon to illuminate her lovely features.

He sat up in bed, stared at her for several minutes, then reached out to touch her hair. Suddenly, there was a bright light outside the window, and a face peered inside at them—it was Ina. In her right hand, she held a revolver, and in the left a burning torch.

"Morgan, I've tied Pearl's feet to the bed, and I've set the house afire," Ina said. In the reality of the dream, Morgan accepted what his wife said, and didn't check for the bonds around Pearl's feet.

"The children's room is already burning," Ina said. "If you hurry, there may still be time to get her untied and get both of you out the front door. If you try to come out this window, I'll shoot you. Just remember, if you choose to save her, the girls will die."

"Ina, how can you do this?"

She ignored his question. "I think I hear them crying, Morgan. Do you hear them?"

"Oh, God, I hear my babies!"

He looked down one last time at Pearl, who, unexplainably, remained asleep. He jumped naked from the bed and ran into the hallway. Behind him, he heard the bedroom door slam shut, followed by the hideous sound of his wife's laughter. Then, Pearl cried out in agony, "Help me, Morgan! I'm burning, I'm burning."

Morgan ran back and turned the knob, but the door would not open. He could feel the heat building on the other side. Inexplicably, his missing limb had been restored, and he began pounding the door with both fists. The heavy oak door would not yield, but he desperately kept pounding, pounding . . .

Morgan awakened, his heart racing and his body drenched in sweat. He glanced wildly across the hotel room, finally assuring himself of his surroundings. He had returned to the waking world, where his nightmare had already come to pass. Pearl, for an all-too-brief moment, had returned to him, but now, the door leading to her was closed forever. For the rest of his life, he would long for another moment with her, but he would never again dream of Pearl.

CHAPTER 14

On Friday morning, the public square was filled with people speculating about the identities of the mystery witnesses Sandusky had announced the night before. Who could these people be, and what bearing would they have on the case? Would they be able to prove that Mrs. Simmons had gotten on the train intending to murder Pearl Owens, and even if the state could prove that she had, would it be reason enough to send the mother of those two lovely children to the electric chair?

The crowd awaiting entrance to the courthouse was even larger than the day before. As the newspaper reporters would remark in their articles, there seemed to be more women in the square than previously, and with all the popcorn and sandwich vendors, the town was taking on a carnival atmosphere. For those who could not find standing room in the courthouse, many of whom had never ventured into Somerset before, there would be shopping, conversation, and other amusements.

Within five minutes after the courthouse doors opened at 8 a.m., all available seats and floor space were occupied. Half a dozen bold young women straddled the banisters between the jury and the audience, and made their way to the judge's bench, where they perched to either side of the platform.

The bailiff had watched the women cross the railing. He asked courtroom guards to help him prevent any more spectators from joining them, but to prevent a possible riot, the guards allowed the initial trespassers to keep their seats.

Before Judge Tartar entered the courtroom at 9 a.m., the bailiff explained to the judge why he should share his bench with his young constituents. Tartar grudgingly agreed—if the spectators remained absolutely silent during the proceedings.

Ina Simmons, wearing a black dress and matching felt hat, entered the courtroom, accompanied by her children, attorneys, and now familiar enclave of close relatives. While the audience whistled and applauded her, Judge Tartar's announced entrance went largely unnoticed. After a minute of pounding his gavel at regular intervals, the judge finally succeeded in calling his court to order.

"I caution all present in this room that I will not tolerate contemptuous behavior in this court, not even if every spectator must be cleared from the room for the remainder of these proceedings," Judge Tartar said.

"I don't see why this case is so different from other cases. The attorneys on both sides have not shown the proper respect for the court, and I am warning the lawyers that if they violate the court's rules of procedure, I will not hesitate to exact the most drastic punishment. It's not fair to the defendant or the Commonwealth. This is a serious case, and the slightest commotion might cause a panic."

This time, at least the crowd took him seriously, but only time would tell if attorneys on both sides would exercise increased restraint. H. C. Kennedy was itching to tell Judge Tartar why this case was so different. It was a rare thing for a woman to be tried for murder in these parts, and this was a crime of passion. Kennedy took the measure of Tartar. Passion between a man and a woman is probably hard for someone like you to fathom, Judge, he thought.

He, as well as most of the people sitting in the courtroom, knew that Judge Tartar had always reserved all of his passion for the Bible, the plays of Shakespeare, the speeches of Cicero, and other classic works in the library. The judge had been married once, but it lasted less than a week, and he had happily returned to his scholarly pursuits.

"The state will now present its next witness," Tartar said.

J. S. Sandusky stood at his table and faced the judge.

"Your honor," he said, "the state rests its case."

There had been no calls in the night from Ina Simmons' attorneys, no indications that she was willing to confess to murder in exchange for a lesser sentence. This indicated to Sandusky that Ina and her husband had probably planned Pearl's murder alone, or spoken about their murder plans only with a close family member, if to anyone else at all.

Once again, conversation spread like wildfire throughout the audience. Judge Tartar pounded his gavel for order, but it took a moment for the tumult to subside.

He looked across the crowded room at the people sitting in the windowsills and even perched like birds on his own bench. These were the people who helped elect him. This multitude of wild, jungle beasts had chosen him as their master of ceremonies for the circus they were trying to turn the trial into. He considered following through with his threat to vacate the room, but changed his mind when calm was restored.

"The defense will now call its first witness," Judge Tartar said.

Defense attorney R. L. Pope paused to adjust his necktie, then, still standing behind his table, addressed the judge.

"Your honor," he said, "with all due respect, the defense requests that the jury be given peremptory instructions to find the defendant not guilty. Defense requests a direct verdict of acquittal on the grounds that the state has not produced a shred of evidence which proves that it was Mrs. Simmons who pulled the trigger on the gun that killed Miss Owens. There has not been sufficient evidence to show that the shots fired caused Miss Owens' death. Furthermore, the Commonwealth has failed to identify the dead woman as Miss Owens."

"Defense's motion is overruled," Judge Tartar said. "The family of Miss Owens identified the woman when they received her body in Louisville. Mr. Pope, call your first witness."

"The defense calls Mrs. Ina Simmons to the stand. In direct testimony, she will give her side of the story."

After being sworn in, Ina began her well-rehearsed testimony.

"I was born in Marshes Creek, McCreary County, and at the age of 17 years, I married Morgan Simmons, then County Clerk and later Circuit Clerk of McCreary County. We have two children. During the first years of our married life, my husband provided well for me. Early last year, our home burned down, and about $600 in insurance money which belonged to me was given to Miss Owens by my husband. My husband gave her money in checks."

"Do you have evidence of these checks?" Pope asked.

"Yes, I have here two checks, one in the amount of $30 and another for $40, both dated May 1928, made payable to Miss Owens and signed by my husband, Morgan Simmons."

Ina Simmons handed the checks to her attorney. "Let the record indicate these two checks which I'm entering into evidence," Pope said. "I will allow the jury to examine these." He handed the checks to the nearest juror, a farmer dressed in a clean pair of coveralls.

"Could you tell us about the fire, Mrs. Simmons?"

"I was not at home when our house was destroyed." Ina wiped away tears with a handkerchief. "All of my clothing and furniture were burned, and it nearly wrecked me."

"By wrecked, I assume that you mean you had an emotional breakdown. Is that correct, Mrs. Simmons?"

"Yes, I had a breakdown. I lost a great deal of weight, and I had to be hospitalized in Lexington for my nerves."

"Was this the first time you had problems with your nerves?"

"No, I had a bad episode years before. My husband and I had domestic trouble prior to my husband's relations with Miss Owens, and I learned he had been unfaithful with other women."

"When did this occur?"

"Just after our second child was born. Morgan often stayed away from home nights before I had her, and things didn't change after she was born. Some friends told me what he'd been doing."

"How did you feel upon learning of Mr. Simmons unfaithfulness?"

"I felt so terrible that I shot myself. This was about six years ago."

"And were you hospitalized at that time?"

"Yes, I had surgery in a Lexington hospital. It took months for me to recover physically, but my nerves never were the same after that."

"How were things in your marriage after your surgery?"

"For a short time after, my husband treated me fine. I worked in his office."

"What were your duties in your husband's office?"

"I was his chief deputy. The chief deputy is supposed to fill in for the clerk of the circuit court any time he has to be away."

"And how often did your husband's job require him to be away?"

"Except for sickness, Morgan had to go to Lexington or Louisville two times a year for a three-day meeting with other clerks from across the state. But during the last year, I had to fill in for him on several occasions. He would disappear for days at a time without letting me know where he had gone."

"Where do you think he was on these days?"

"I don't have any doubt that he was with Miss Owens."

"Objection," Sandusky said. "Calls for speculation on the witness' part."

"Sustained," Judge Tartar said.

"Where did your family stay after the fire that destroyed your house?"

"After our home had burned, we stayed at a hotel for a short time and then rented a house."

"Did your husband stay there with you and your daughters?"

"Sometimes. At that time my husband would leave home for a week or a few days at a time, and I didn't know where he was."

"Mrs. Simmons, when did you first hear of Pearl Decker Owens?"

"I first learned my husband was going with Miss Owens about a year before her death. A friend of mine in Danville told me she had seen my husband and a woman sitting close together on the train. I took the matter up with Mr. Simmons, and he denied having illicit relations with Miss Owens. He said they were just friends who ran into each other occasionally."

"So your husband openly discussed his acquaintance with Miss Owens?"

"No. After this he became cold, indifferent and crabby, and as days went along, our domestic trouble grew worse."

"Did you believe him when he told you there was nothing going on between them?"

"I wanted to with all my heart, and I kept my spirits up pretty well, considering the way he was acting towards me. Then, Miss Owens called me over the telephone on December 24, 1927 and said, 'I am mad at Morgan and I'm not going to spend Christmas with him in Danville.'

"I—almost lost my mind after that call." Ina's voice remained calm, but a steady stream of tears began rolling down her cheeks. "When I heard her voice, I knew that there really had been something going on between them. I had another breakdown. Dr. Blain, my family doctor in Whitley City, sent me to Lexington for observation. I spent a week there, trying to recover from what that phone call had done to me."

Pope looked to the jury for their reaction. Several of the men were shaking their heads; a couple of elderly jurors were wiping at tears with the backs of their hands. Pope smiled; she was breaking their hearts.

"How was your general condition affected as a result of this episode?"

"I was always on edge after I returned home. A few months before I went into the hospital, I weighed 135. I weighed 102 when I got out."

"How did your husband act toward you after you returned from the hospital?"

"He started acting better towards me. For a short time after this, he treated me all right."

"Was this the last time you spoke on the phone with Miss Owens?"

"No. At another time, Miss Owens called the offices of my husband, while I was in the room. I answered the phone . . .'"

"Hello," Ina said.

"Is—Morgan there?" a feminine voice asked, apparently surprised that a woman had answered the phone.

"He is," Ina said. "May I ask who's calling?"

"Tell him it's Pearl," the voice replied.

"Morgan, your ex-lover wants to speak to you," Ina said, making no effort to cover the receiver.

"I'm not going to talk to her." Morgan stared at the papers on his desk.

"Don't let me stop you. You told me you were through with her; here's your chance to tell her again."

Morgan ignored Ina and returned to his receipt book.

"He doesn't want to speak with you," Ina said, "but I'd be glad to chat awhile."

"Tell him it's very important that we talk," Pearl said.

"I don't think that would make a bit of difference to him. Can't you get it through your head that he's through with you?"

"Through with me? Mrs. Simmons, he's anything but through with me. It's only a matter of time until I move in with Morgan and the kids.

Sleeping over gave me a real liking for the place."

"What are you talking about?"

"I'm saying you've got a real comfortable bed. I slept in it while you were in the hospital, and a couple of times more after that." Pearl laughed.

"You're lying!" Ina said. "You've never been in my house. God as my witness, you never will!"

"Ask the little girl next door if you don't believe me. Better yet, ask your sweet little girls about their momma's friend."

After delivering her final jab, Pearl hung up before Ina could respond . . .

"How did you feel upon learning of your husband's continued infidelity?" Pope asked.

"I went all to pieces. It hurt so much, to learn she had been in my bed with my husband while I was lying in that hospital, fighting for my sanity."

"How did your husband respond?"

He wouldn't respond at all to the things she had said. He started treating me cold again, and ignoring me, the way he had before I was hospitalized in Lexington."

"Had you ever seen Miss Owens on any occasion before you saw her on the train on August 9, 1928?"

"On June first, last year, I went to a hotel in Lexington, where my husband was registered. I knocked on his door and a woman answered, saying she was the maid and that Mr. Simmons hadn't been in the room. Later, I learned the woman was Miss Owens."

"Was this the only time you saw her?"

"No. A month later, on July first, I was in Lexington again to find out if my husband was there with Miss Owens. He told me, when he left home, that he was going to Tennessee, and I had learned that he did not take that train. In Lexington, I found he had registered at a hotel, but there was no one in his room. I saw Miss Owens on the mezzanine floor. I followed her out onto the street, where I talked to her, and then we went up to his room, where she told me everything.

"Miss Owens said Mr. Simmons had told her that he was not living with me. I asked Miss Owens to leave him alone because we were still living together. Miss Owens said that Mr. Simmons had bought her furs, and all the diamonds she was wearing that day, and she wanted to know how much money he made. I told her about $100 a month, and she said that my husband had furnished her more than that."

"Where do you think your husband could have gotten the extra money?"

"Two places. He told me he hadn't received the insurance money, but as I learned later, he had already received my share of the money from the house fire and had spent it on things for her.

"That was bad enough, but as I told her, Morgan had been indicted in June for embezzling state and county funds. When the indictment came out, I was so ashamed, I couldn't show my face in public. Since I worked in the same office, people probably thought I had been in on it with him."

Pope turned to glance at the jury. Again, several of the jurors were shaking their heads in sympathy.

"What did your husband do with the money?"

"I didn't know anything about any money. I assume he used it to buy fancy clothes and jewels for Miss Owens. I know I wouldn't have been standing in front of her in a gingham dress if he'd spent any of it on me."

"Did you see your husband on the July visit to Lexington?"

"Yes. I saw him outside in the hallway and asked him what he had to say about it. He said 'Nothing.' Right there in front of him, Miss Owens promised not to have anything more to do with my husband, and I went on home."

"Did you say anything to Miss Owens before you left Lexington?"

"Yes. I told her that I forgave her, and that I believed she would not have had anything to do with my husband if she had known he had been lying to her."

"In other words, you did not hold any malice in your heart towards Miss Owens after you had your talk with her?"

"None whatsoever. My heart was unburdened for the first time in all the months that I had known about her."

"Did your husband return with you from Lexington?"

"No. I saw Mr. Simmons the next morning back in Whitley City, and we went back to housekeeping. I thought the trouble was over."

"But your troubles were not over, were they Mrs. Simmons?"

"No. A little over a month later, last August, my husband rushed in with a telegram and said he had business in Somerset. I asked him if he was telling the truth. He gave me the telegram and told me I could verify it by the operator.

"I saw the operator, and she told me the telegram came for my husband. Later, after I explained to her what had been going on between Morgan and me, the operator told me it was a fake and that my husband practically forced her to write it."

"What did you do upon learning that the telegram had been faked?"

"I decided to go looking for him and catch him in his lie. I borrowed a dress, hat, and a hatbox from my neighbor, Miss Catherine Williams, and then I took a taxi to Stearns."

"Why did you borrow the dress, hat, and hatbox from Miss Williams?"

"I didn't have anything decent to wear, and if I had to see Miss Owens again, I wanted to be dressed as nice as she had been the last time I saw her."

"And the hatbox?"

"I carried one of my husband's pistols in the box after I put the hat on."

"Mrs. Simmons, why did you carry a concealed pistol on the train with you? Did you have plans to use it on either Miss Owens or your husband?"

"Absolutely not. I didn't take it with me to harm anyone. I've always carried a pistol with me every time I've travelled alone. I didn't have room in my purse for the pistol, so I thought the hatbox would be a safe place for it."

"Are you saying you had a purse with you on the train? We have heard patrolman Matney testify that he did not find a purse."

"I know I had one with me in the taxi, and when I paid for my ticket at Stearns. I . . . don't remember if I had it after I changed trains in Danville."

"How long have you been acquainted with guns, Mrs. Simmons?"

"Ever since I was a little girl growing up on the farm. My daddy always said they wouldn't be a danger to us unless we didn't know how to handle them. And my husband always had several guns around the house after we were married."

"Miss Williams has testified that you told her you were going to take the train to Danville, yet she saw you taking a taxi in the opposite direction."

"Yes, I had the taxi take me to the coal shute at Stearns. I knew that I could get on the train when it stopped there to take on coal and water."

"But why didn't you catch the train at the depot in Whitley City?"

"I didn't want anyone there sending my husband word that I was coming looking for him. After what he had done with the telegraph operator in Whitley City, I didn't know who I could trust."

"Why did you think your husband would be in Danville with Miss Owens? Since he had lied about being called away to Somerset on the telegram, couldn't he have been headed somewhere else, like Lexington or Louisville?"

"He could have been, but I checked his closet before I went to talk to the telegraph operator. Usually, he would take at least one extra suit if he went to Lexington or Louisville, but all of his suits were there, except for the one he was wearing when he left that morning."

"What did that tell you, Mrs. Simmons?"

"I figured since he only had the one suit, he was planning to meet her in Danville for an overnight stay. That was where she'd planned to meet him that Christmas, and it was kind of a half-way meeting point, between Whitley City and Louisville."

"Did you take any extra clothing with you?"

"No, I hadn't planned on being gone long enough to change outfits."

"But what if you had had to go all the way to Lexington or Louisville looking for him?"

"I was too upset to think about that at the time. I just had a strong hunch that he would be in Danville."

"Did you see your husband there?"

"No, but when the train pulled up in Danville, I saw Miss Owens outside the depot, smoking a cigarette in the breezeway. When she got on the southbound train, I followed, but I didn't see my husband. I went to sleep on the seat, and when I woke up, I saw Miss Owens with her arm around my husband's neck. I don't remember anything more until after the shooting."

"You don't remember removing your husband's gun from the hatbox, or pointing it at Miss Owens?"

"No, something snapped in my brain, and I don't remember anything until a policeman told me I was under arrest and put me in a patrol car at Ferguson."

"Do you remember anyone asking you questions before you were placed in the car?"

"No, I don't remember anyone asking questions."

"Mrs. Simmons, where is your home?"

"I haven't any home now. Since that night in August, I've been living with my mother and father in Junction City."

"And what about your daughters? Where do they live?"

"They live with a neighbor in Whitley City. I felt it was important for them to continue in the same school, so I only see them on weekends."

"I have no further questions for the witness, your honor," Pope said.

"It's now 11:30," Judge Tartar said. "Court will recess for lunch until 1 p.m., at which time the State may question this witness."

The judge, attorneys, and Ina and her family exited via the anteroom. As they had the day before, more than 100 spectators, fearful of losing their seats, ate bag lunches in the courtroom during the recess.

CHAPTER 15

Promptly, at one o'clock, Judge Tartar returned, and court was called to order.

"The State may question the witness," Judge Tartar said.

Prosecuting attorney J.S. Sandusky rose from his chair, walked over to pick up something from the evidence table, and then approached Ina at the witness stand.

"Miss Owens, you have shown us two checks from your husband made out to Miss Owens which total a mere $70." Sandusky waved the checks before the jury. "Do you have any receipts which would indicate that your husband purchased clothing or jewelry for her, as you have indicated she told you?"

"No, those two checks are all the receipts I have."

"Do you have any idea why your husband wrote these checks to Miss Owens?"

"No, but I can guess,"

"Guessing is not good enough, Mrs. Simmons. Could the money have been for repayment of a loan?"

"No, because Miss Owens told me that my husband had been giving her money."

"Was there anyone else who heard Miss Owens tell you that Mr. Simmons had purchased items for her or given her money?"

"No. No one else was present in the room."

"Since Miss Owens is no longer with us to verify what you say, the jury must accept your word in this matter. Isn't that correct, Mrs. Simmons?"

"Yes, I suppose it is."

Sandusky paused, walked to his table, and thumbed through a legal pad.

"Mrs. Simmons, you testified that when your possessions were destroyed in the house fire, and I quote, 'it nearly wrecked me.' You admitted to Mr.

Pope that you suffered a breakdown and had to be hospitalized in Lexington, during which time you lost a great deal of weight."

"Yes, that is what I said."

"Were you hospitalized before or after your house burned?"

"Before. I was in the hospital in February, and our house burned in March."

"So you experienced the trauma of losing all of your belongings after you returned from the hospital?"

"Yes."

"Did you resent Miss Owens for her fine clothing when you saw her in July?"

"Not until she told me where her money came from. After that, I couldn't help but feel hurt."

"But you testified that you forgave her after she told you your husband had lied to her?"

"Yes, I totally forgave her."

"And you believed her when she said she promised she would leave your husband alone?"

"I believed her."

"Did you have any reason to believe she had lied to you between the time you saw her on July first and the early morning of August 10, when you saw her beside your husband on the train?"

"Not until my husband handed me the fake telegram."

"So it was your husband who gave you reason to doubt Mrs. Owens' promise?"

"Yes."

"And no one told you Miss Owens was going to meet your husband on the train?"

"That is correct."

"Then why do you think you got so angry at Miss Owens when you saw her sitting next to him on the train?"

"She had her arms around his neck!"

Sandusky fought to stifle a grin. He had hit a nerve.

"Mrs. Simmons, I understand the defense has been unable to find anyone on that train who saw Miss Owens with her arms around your husband. Several people saw them sitting together for the two miles the train had traveled from Somerset to Ferguson, but no one remembers seeing them embracing."

"I know what I saw."

"For all you know, Miss Pearl Owens kept her promise to you and didn't know she would run into your husband on the train as it passed through Somerset."

"She said she would leave my husband alone, but she had her arms around him." Ina's voice was tinged with anger.

"But up until that moment, you must admit she had kept her promise."

"As far as I know."

"Your husband told the press that Miss Owens had a telegram with her from one of her sisters which indicated she was on her way to meet them and her little boy in Tennessee. Mrs. Owens' sisters have confirmed that they did send her such a telegram. Therefore, it would seem that Miss Owens had a legitimate reason for being on the train, other than to meet your husband."

"Objection, your honor," Kennedy said. "Mr. Sandusky is speculating. Does he have a question for my client?"

"Mr. Sandusky?" Judge Tartar asked.

"Yes, your honor, if the court will bear with me, I am leading up to a question. Mrs. Simmons, since Mr. Simmons got on the train in Somerset that night, there is nothing to indicate that he had faked his telegram that morning, is there?"

"The woman at the telegraph office told me she had faked it."

"Have either you or your attorneys been able to locate this alleged telegraph operator?"

"No, we haven't."

"Neither has the state, Mrs. Simmons. Was the fake telegram your idea or your husband's?"

"I have no idea what you're talking about."

"Did you see your husband get the train in Somerset?"

"No, I didn't."

"Are you always such a sound sleeper, Mrs. Simmons? Trains usually make a lot of noise when they pull into a station."

"I was suffering from nervous exhaustion, so I slept much sounder."

"Mrs. Simmons, did you borrow clothing from anyone for your trips to Lexington on June first and July first?"

"No. I didn't."

"What did you wear on those two occasions?"

"One of my gingham dresses, I suppose."

"But they were no longer good enough for you to wear in August when you went looking for your husband on the train?" Sandusky moved closer to intimidate Ina.

"I didn't want Miss Owens to see me the way she had seen me before. I wanted her to see that I could dress up and look as nice as she had the last time I had seen her."

"In other words, you expected to see Miss Owens that day, and you felt you were competing with her?"

"I didn't know I would run into her. I just didn't want to look inferior to her—in the event we met again."

"Since you were dressed so nicely in August, why didn't you go up to Miss Owens and speak with her on the train when you saw her in Danville? At this point, for all you knew, she had kept her promise to stay away from your husband."

"I just didn't feel like talking to her."

"But you did feel like riding behind her for the 44 miles between Danville and Somerset, waiting until you could find an excuse to kill her, didn't you, Mrs. Simmons?"

"Objection," Pope said. "Mr. Sandusky is trying to create his own scenario."

Judge Tartar sustained.

Sandusky stopped long enough to pull a handkerchief from his pants pocket and wipe the sweat from his brow, then continued.

"You didn't have your husband's pistol in Miss Williams' hatbox, did you, Mrs. Simmons?"

"Yes, as I told Mr. Pope and the jury, I did."

"Your husband passed the pistol to you when he walked from the rear to the center of the car, didn't he?"

Sandusky's unexpected accusation ignited heated discussions all across the courtroom. Judge Tartar pounded his gavel and demanded order. Finally, the din subsided, and Ina responded.

"No. I told you I was asleep and didn't see him get on the train."

Sandusky walked closer to Ina. He placed his right hand on the witness stand and stared straight into her eyes.

"Mr. Simmons spoke to you about Miss Owens after you saw her on July first in Lexington, didn't he?"

"No, he never would mention her, not before or after I caught her in his room."

"He told you that she was still asking to see him, didn't he?"

"No, he didn't."

"He told you he didn't feel anything for her, but Miss Owens was still in love with him. He was afraid that if he ended things with her, she would testify in his embezzlement trial and account for a lot of the missing money."

Sandusky paused and looked into Ina's eyes for a sign that she was about to crack under the strain—there was none. "Isn't that so?"

"I don't know what you're talking about."

"Morgan Simmons convinced you that the only way he could stay out of prison and return to you and your children was if you killed Miss Owens for him, didn't he?"

"No, he didn't say any such thing!" Ina finally raised her voice.

Sandusky caught a glimpse of fire in her eyes and applied more kindling.

"Isn't it true that you killed Miss Owens to protect your husband?"

"Something must have snapped in me when I saw her with him that way!"

"Your defense counsel wants us to believe that you were momentarily seized by an insane, primitive impulse to protect your babies and your home, but the fact of the matter is that you loved your husband enough to kill for him, didn't you?"

"No. That's not true." Ina had regained her composure. "I didn't plan what happened."

"You loved him enough to shoot yourself when you were afraid you were going to lose him six years ago, and he knew you still loved him enough to kill to keep him, didn't he?"

"Objection!" Pope said. "Mrs. Simmons has already replied to this. How many times must she answer the same question?"

"Sustained," Judge Tartar said.

"You never forgave Miss Owens for receiving the things your husband foolishly bought for her with your insurance money, did you?"

"Yes, I told you I did." Ina's face exuded serenity.

"Your husband told you Pearl Owens would be getting on the train in Danville, and he told you to sit close to her in disguise, didn't he?"

"He did not." Tears suddenly gleamed in her eyes.

"He handed you the gun, didn't he?"

"He did not." A single tear rolled down her cheek, but she stared Sandusky in the eye and remained outwardly calm.

"And you remember standing up in the aisle, placing the gun at the back of her head, and pulling the trigger, don't you?"

"I don't remember any of that."

"You remember firing two times into Miss Pearl Decker Owens, don't you?"

"I don't remember. I don't remember." By now, tears were rolling down her cheeks, but she hadn't waivered. She had subdued her rage.

"You are a cold one, Mrs. Simmons." Sandusky was frustrated by his inability to pressure Ina into a confession. "Your honor, I have no further questions for the witness."

"The witness is now excused," Judge Tartar said.

Ina's attorney, Pope, helped her down from the witness stand and escorted her to her chair. Then, he called Somerset physician W. R. Cardin. An elderly gentleman rose to take the stand.

"Dr. Cardin, what was the nature of your relationship with Mrs. Ina Simmons?" Pope asked.

The grey-haired gentleman peered over his wire-rimmed spectacles and said, "I delivered both of her daughters in my office here in Somerset. Saw the little girls for yearly checkups, shots and such. I tended to her after her suicide attempt about six years ago."

"How would you describe Mrs. Simmons' health after the birth of each of her children, and after the suicide attempt?"

"She was only about eighteen years of age when I delivered her first child. Mrs. Simmons was a picture of health, and there were no complications with the birth."

"How would you describe her mental health at that time?"

"She was happy and excited, like most first-time mothers are. She was looking forward to raising her child."

"How would you describe Mrs. Simmons at the time her second child was born?"

"She was a changed woman. Physically, she was in good health, and there were no problems with the birth, but she seemed depressed. She told me her husband had been leaving her home alone a lot while she was pregnant, and she had been quite depressed as a result of this during the last trimester."

"When did you next see Mrs. Simmons after the birth?"

"It was only a few months later. She had shot herself, and been operated on in Lexington to repair the damage. Her family doctor in Whitley City felt it would be good for her to come to me for additional care."

"What was the nature of this care?"

"Mostly, I monitored her progress from her surgery in Lexington. She was terribly slow to heal, and for a long time her doctors, myself among them, were afraid she still was going to die."

"Why were you so concerned?"

"It seemed she had lost the will to recover. I believe the mind plays a big part in the mending process."

"Were you able to treat her for her depression?"

"No. I felt Dr. Hamlin in Burnside would be better. He is more experienced in dealing with emotional and mental problems."

"No further questions for the witness," said Pope.

"State's witness," Judge Tartar said.

"Dr. Cardin," Sandusky asked, "am I correct in assuming that you did not treat Mrs. Simmons further after you referred her to Dr. Hamlin?"

"Yes, that's correct."

"Therefore, you are unaware of her mental and physical condition in recent years, namely since her home burned and after she learned of her husband's alleged involvement with Pearl Owens?"

"She hasn't been to see me in recent years."

"I have no further questions for this witness, your honor."

Sandusky glanced at the defense table as he walked back to his chair. The accused woman held the same detached expression she had worn during most of the trial. Her oldest child chomped on a stick of gum and fidgeted in her chair. The youngest daughter lay asleep across her mother's lap.

Dr. Cardin was excused, and the defense called T. L. Hamlin, a physician from the nearby community of Burnside.

"Dr. Hamlin, could you describe your professional relationship with Mrs. Simmons?" Pope asked.

The doctor stroked his long black beard with his right hand, as if the gesture might help him to remember. Momentarily, he replied, "I believe Mrs. Simmons was referred to my practice about six years ago by Dr. Blain of Somerset. She had been severely depressed as a result of domestic problems."

"You specialize in the treatment of mental illness?"

"Yes."

"How severe was Mrs. Simmons' depression?"

"She complained of being unable to sleep and having a poor appetite. As a result, she often found herself in tears at the slightest provocation."

"Were you eventually able to help her with her problem?"

"Yes, over time her mental outlook improved somewhat, but I don't believe I can say that she ever fully recovered emotionally after her suicide attempt."

"What do you think brought about this degree of improvement in her condition?"

"I believe the most important thing in Mrs. Simmons' life was always maintaining a happy married and home life. When she reached the point where her husband seemed to be remaining faithful to her, she became a different person. I can't say she was happy, but she seemed able to cope with her life. I decided I had accomplished enough to discharge her from my care."

"But she did return to your office later, did she not?"

"Yes, she returned about two years ago. Her depression had returned, and she was much as she had been after her suicide attempt."

"Did she tell you what was troubling her?"

"She said her husband was spending a lot of time away from home again. She suspected that he was seeing someone else. By January of last year, she said she had proof of her suspicions."

"You are referring to a phone call she received from Miss Owens at her home?"

"Yes. She mentioned the conversation and the effect it was having on her . . ."

Ina sat gripping the padded leather arms of a chair in Dr. Hamlin's office. Hamlin sat on the opposite side of his oak desk.

"How have you felt since talking with this woman on the telephone,

Mrs. Simmons?"

"I haven't had a full night's sleep since it happened. I can't stand the sight of food, and I—I hate to say this, doctor, but I'm hateful with the children over the slightest thing."

"You really love your children, don't you, Mrs. Simmons?" Dr. Hamlin asked.

"With all my heart." Tears were forming in her eyes.

"Would it not be in their best interests if you could leave your present relationship with Mr. Simmons? It's obvious that you can't make Mr. Simmons change his ways. Perhaps the best thing you can do for yourself and your children is to divorce your husband and start anew."

"Don't even suggest such a thing!" Her tears started flowing. "Morgan Simmons is the father of my babies. He belongs to me, and nothing that he does is ever going to change that. For better or worse, he will always be my husband . . ."

"During any of her visits to your office," Pope asked, "did Mrs. Simmons ever make any threats toward Miss Owens or her husband? Did she ever say she wanted to hurt either of them or wished they were dead?"

"She never made any such comments. Her nerves were tormenting her, and she blamed her troubles on what her husband was doing, but I never heard her threaten or wish ill towards anyone."

"Why do you think she reacted as she did towards Miss Owens on the train?"

"I've treated several thousand mental cases, and I'm positive that Mrs. Simmons didn't know what she was doing when she killed Miss Owens, if indeed she did commit the act. You have to realize that Mrs. Simmons had been under stress for the past six years, and under an unbelievable amount for the last two years. No one could have predicted how that stress would be released."

"Defense has no further questions for the witness," Pope said.

"State's witness," Judge Tartar said.

"Dr. Hamlin, who do you think Mrs. Simmons blamed for the stress and agony you described?" Sandusky asked.

"She felt her husband was responsible."

"Then, why didn't she shoot her husband instead of Miss Owens?"

"I don't think anyone on this earth can say why. I do believe that Mrs. Simmons always loved her husband, no matter what he might have done to her."

"In your professional opinion, did she love her husband enough to commit murder for him?"

"Objection!" Pope said.

"Overruled," Judge Tartar said. "The witness will answer the question."

"I don't believe anyone in my profession could answer that."

"Dr. Hamlin, in your testimony to Mr. Pope, you expressed some doubt as to whether Mrs. Simmons did indeed murder Miss Owens. Do you have information linking someone else to the crime?" Sandusky asked.

"Not at all, but I understand that no one actually saw her shoot the woman."

"Dr. Hamlin, have you spoken with Mr. Morgan Simmons in recent weeks?"

"Yes. He came to me a few days ago and asked if I would be willing to testify at this trial."

At this point, several people in the audience began talking among themselves; most of the townsfolk had heard of and wondered about the significance of Morgan's visits to Dr. Hamlin and other area physicians.

"Did he tell you why he wanted you to testify?"

"He wanted the jury to know that his wife had not been mentally well at the time the crime was committed."

"Do you believe a mentally disturbed individual would be more likely than a sane or mentally healthy individual to murder someone in the way that Miss Owens was slain?"

"Yes, I believe that would be more likely."

"Based upon your recent conversations with him, do you believe Mr. Simmons is a sane individual?"

"Yes, based upon the very limited discussion we had, there didn't appear to be anything wrong with his mental state."

"Therefore, if both Mr. Simmons and his wife had been suspected of this crime, Mrs. Simmons would have been the most likely suspect, in your professional opinion?"

"Objection, your honor!" Pope said before Dr. Hamlin could answer. "Calls for speculation on the part of the witness."

"Overruled. The witness will answer the question."

"Based upon my limited impression of Mr. Simmons, since I've not examined him for emotional problems, I would have to give you a tentative yes."

"How convenient for Mr. Simmons that you are here today to relieve him of suspicion, and direct it instead to his wife, who as mother to two young children, will be treated with more sympathy," Sandusky said.

"Objection!" Pope said. "Defense requests that Mr. Sandusky's statements be stricken."

Judge Tartar sustained. "The jury will disregard Mr. Sandusky's last remarks."

"I have no further questions for the witness," Sandusky said.

After Dr. Hamlin was excused, the defense called Dr. W. L. Kaiser. After the parade of elderly and middle-aged physicians who had testified, many in the audience were surprised when a young man with dark wavy hair and a narrow black mustache took the stand.

"Dr. Kaiser, how long have you known Mrs. Simmons?" Pope asked.

"Some five or six years. I'm on staff at Lexington General, where Mrs. Simmons was brought for treatment of a gunshot wound to the abdomen. After a staff surgeon completed her surgery, I was referred to begin counseling sessions with her."

"How was Mrs. Simmons affected, physically and emotionally, by her operation?"

"The surgery was quite serious. It took months for her to heal. The long recovery process alone would have depressed anybody. Physical activities are severely limited for quite some time after such surgery."

"Was Mr. Simmons with his wife in the hospital?"

"Yes. He sat in on several counseling sessions. He openly accepted responsibility for driving his wife to attempt to commit suicide and promised to treat her better."

"How long did you treat Mrs. Simmons after the surgery?"

"Only until she was well enough to travel back home. Because of the great distances involved, I recommended she continue to see someone closer to her home. I understand that she began seeing Dr. Hamlin in Burnside on a regular basis."

"Did you see Mrs. Simmons on any other occasion?"

"Yes. Dr. Hamlin called me last February, about a year ago now. He said Mrs. Simmons' emotional problems had returned, so he felt I should take another look at her. Her sister brought her to the hospital in Lexington; after examining Mrs. Simmons, I decided to hospitalize her."

"What was her condition at that time?"

"She was quite thin, and severely depressed. I admitted her to the hospital for one week of treatment."

"Did her condition improve during that week?"

"Enough that I felt she could return home and at least cope with daily life. When she was admitted, she was on the verge of a total collapse."

"In other words, Mrs. Simmons was not what we would call mentally well when she returned home."

"That is correct."

"Dr. Kaiser, if indeed Mrs. Simmons did shoot Miss Owens, why would she have done so? Had she expressed any animosity, or made any threats toward Miss Owens?"

"None at all. I don't believe she knew what she was doing, or that she had the will of control to prevent it. I believe that over the years, the trauma of her operation eventually built up until it caused an insane impulse in Mrs. Simmons which led to the shooting."

"So you don't believe Mrs. Simmons should be held accountable for what she might have done while possessed of this insane impulse?"

"I don't think she should be."

"Thank you, Dr. Kaiser. I have no further questions for the witness," Pope said.

"State's witness," said Judge Tartar.

"Dr. Kaiser, were you present on the train the night of August 9, 1928, when Miss Owens was murdered?" Sandusky asked.

"No, I was not."

"So you cannot be absolutely certain what Mrs. Simmons' mental state was at that time, can you?"

"Taking the degree of her previous mental problems into consideration, I can state with a high level of probability that she entered into a state of momentary insanity when she saw Miss Owens with her arms around Mr. Simmons."

"Dr. Kaiser, I didn't ask you for probabilities or a hypothesis. You do not know for certain that she was insane at a moment when you were not present to observe her, do you?"

"No," Kaiser nervously rubbed an index finger over one side of his mustache. "But I—"

"I have your answer," Sandusky said. "Would you have released Mrs. Simmons from your care if you believed she could have harmed herself or anyone else?"

"Certainly, I would not have." The young doctor resented Sandusky, the town of Somerset, the sweltering courtroom, and the fact that the threat of a subpoena was the only reason he had agreed to come all the way from Lexington to testify.

"So this 'insane impulse' which you describe would have been a sudden thing, something which you could not have foreseen?"

"No . . ." Kaiser's mind was more on his train ride home than on Sandusky's question. "I could not have suspected it, but at the same time, I'm not surprised by it. Her background would have made her more susceptible to such an impulse than a sane individual would have been."

"Again, how convenient for Mrs. Simmons, and especially for Mr. Simmons."

"Objection!" Pope said. "I resent Mr. Sandusky's repeated implications that my client was coerced into committing murder by her husband. There is absolutely no evidence to support such an outrageous contention."

"Sustained," Judge Tartar said. "The jury will disregard Mr. Sandusky's last comments."

"I have no further questions for the witness," Sandusky said.

After Dr. Kaiser was excused, the defense called Dr. C. E. Blain of Whitley City. A tall, overweight, middle-aged man responded.

"Dr. Blain, how long have you known Mrs. Simmons?" Pope asked.

"I've been her family physician since just before she was married."

"Then you have been treating her for over ten years."

"Yes, I've seen her and her children several times each year."

"How would you say that Mrs. Simmons has changed, both physically and mentally, in the years that you have known her?"

"Before her first child, and shortly thereafter, she was very strong, happy and healthy. While she was pregnant with the second child, she came in frequently for her nerves. Shortly after the baby was born, she was rushed to my home with a serious gunshot wound . . ."

Dr. C. E. Blain was awakened at 3 a.m. by what sounded like someone trying to kick his front door down. He hurriedly put on his trousers and ran down the stairs.

"Open up! Please, God, open up!" shouted a voice outside his door.

Dr. Blain unlocked and opened the door, and Morgan Simmons rushed in, nearly knocking the doctor to the floor. He was followed by another man who carried Ina, bleeding and unconscious, in his arms.

"What's wrong with her?" Blain asked.

"She shot herself!" Morgan replied.

"Let's get her on the kitchen table," Dr. Blain told Morgan's neighbor. The doctor rushed ahead of them, turning on lights in the hall and kitchen.

As the men placed Ina on the kitchen table, Dr. Blain left the room, then returned with his black medical bag, and a blanket and pillow from a hall closet.

"When did this happen?" Blain asked. He placed the pillow under the unconscious woman.

"Just a few minutes ago," Morgan replied. "This is all my fault. God help me, I drove her to this."

"Looks like she's lost a lot of blood," Blain replied. He covered Ina's legs with the blanket.

"Is she going to make it, Doc?" Morgan asked. "Please tell me she's going to be ok."

"If I can get the bleeding stopped, and if she doesn't go into shock," Blain said. He hurriedly applied gauze to the bullet wound in Ina's abdomen . . .

"You obviously successfully treated the wound," Pope said.

"I stopped the bleeding, but we had to drive her to the hospital in Somerset to have the bullet removed. From there, they sent her to Lexington General for more delicate surgical procedures."

"Did you see her after she returned home?"

"Yes. She was still having trouble with her nerves. I understand Dr. Hamlin was treating her in Burnside, but I saw her on several occasions for checkups and when she would bring her children in."

"How had she changed?"

"She had lost a lot of weight, and looked really pale and fragile."

"When was the last time you saw her?"

"She came in for some nerve medicine last July. She said she couldn't wait until her scheduled visit to Dr. Hamlin's office. I called him, and he told me what to prescribe for her."

"Did she tell you what was troubling her?"

"Yes. I believe she said her husband was seeing some city woman from Louisville, and it was about to tear her apart. She said she couldn't sleep for crying about what Morgan was doing to her."

"Objection to the term 'city woman,' your honor," Sandusky said. "And hearsay is not admissible. The fact that Miss Owens was from Louisville has been made common knowledge in the press."

"Sustained," Judge Tartar said.

"Did she say anything to you about wanting to hurt her husband or anyone else?"

"No, she didn't."

"I have no further questions for the witness," Pope said.

"State's witness," the judge said.

"Dr. Blain," Sandusky asked, "is it true that you didn't treat Mrs. Simmons for her mental problems after she started seeing Dr. Hamlin, except, that is, for calling him about a prescription for her?"

"That is correct."

"Did you see her for physical examinations during the time she was being treated by Dr. Hamlin?"

"Yes. I gave her a standard check-up each year."

"Did you find any physical illness during any of these examinations?"

"Her weight had dropped considerably."

"But there were no illness, no apparent physical problems remaining from the gunshot wound?"

"No, she didn't complain of any problems related to the surgery."

"So, other than being a few pounds lighter than previously, Mrs. Simmons was physically in good health the last time you examined her, Dr. Blain?"

"Yes, but she had lost more than just a few pounds."

"But you could find no physical cause for the weight loss, and she was essentially still physically healthy?"

"Yes, but she did not look healthy."

"But health cannot always be judged by appearances, can it, doctor?"

"No, it cannot."

"I have no further questions for the witness." Sandusky said.

Dr. Blain was excused, and the defense called Dr. C. B. Hall, a dentist from Somerset. He testified that he had seen Mrs. Simmons in his office at least once for each of the last five years, and during each of these years, it appeared that she had lost more weight.

Under cross examination, Sandusky pointed out that dentists are not qualified to assess the psychological and physical conditions of their patients, but he realized that Hall's testimony had added support to the defense's assertion. If the jury believed that declining body weight equaled declining physical health, the series of doctors would have provided ample evidence for Ina's assertion that she had experienced a long, steady physical decline. His greatest fear now was that the jury would agree that Ina's mental competency had declined along with her physical body; therefore, she probably should not be held responsible for her actions.

Judge Tartar excused the witness, and then glanced at his watch. It was nearly 5 p.m. Just as he was about to adjourn for supper, there was a sudden disturbance behind the railing directly in front of the judge's bench. Police Chief Warren, who had been watching the audience carefully all during the trial, jumped over the rail toward a woman who had just sprung from her seat.

The woman, Mrs. Scott Tate of Wyborg in McCreary County, had pulled a pistol from her bosom and pointed it toward Mrs. Frank Ballou of Cumberland Falls. Before Mrs. Tate could take aim, Chief Warren wrestled the gun from her and placed her under temporary arrest. As members of the audience began asking their neighbors if they had seen what had happened, Judge Tartar pounded his gavel for order, and Chief Warren ushered Mrs. Tate into the anteroom.

Chief Warren later told the press that he would take Mrs. Tate before the Grand Jury over the matter, but reporters could only speculate about a possible connection between the dispute of the two women and the murder trial in progress.

Attorney H. C. Kennedy, like Judge Tartar, had seen what had happened, and feared the possible impact it would have upon the jury. He jumped from his chair and said, "Your honor, the defense requests that the jury members not be told any details of the incident which has just transpired behind them, on grounds that it might in some way detrimentally influence their verdict in this case."

"It will be so ordered," Judge Tartar said. "Guards, see to it that no one speaks to the jury about this matter. This court will now adjourn for the evening meal until 6:30 p.m."

CHAPTER 16

The majority of the excited crowd exited the hot, musty courtroom, and again, scores of spectators guarded their choice seats and ate sandwiches from paper bags.

When the trial resumed, the defense called Mrs. Susan Barton of Wilmore, Kentucky to the stand. The tall, fashionably dressed brunette, approximately thirty years old, was sworn in.

"Mrs. Barton, what is your relationship to the accused?" Pope asked.

"She is my sister."

"I understand that you have not lived in the same household since your sister moved out of the paternal residence to marry Morgan Simmons. Is that correct?"

"Yes, it is."

"Have you and your sister remained in close contact during the past ten years?"

"Yes, we have. We visit each other right often, and write letters and talk on the telephone at least twice a month."

"Over the course of the years, has your sister confided in you about the intimate details of her marriage with Morgan Simmons?"

"Yes, I believe she's kept me up on about everything that has happened."

"How would you describe the history of your sister's marriage to Mr. Simmons?"

"Well, in the beginning, my family really thought highly of Morgan. He had a good job at the courthouse, and we thought he really loved Ina. We had heard rumors that he was stepping out on Ina after their first girl was born, but nobody ever said a word to Ina about it. While she was carrying the second baby, Ina told me that Morgan was hardly ever home with her.

"She called me in tears one night after somebody in Whitley City told her that they had seen Morgan out with several different women late at night. She told me she couldn't figure what she'd done wrong, and didn't know what she could do to change things. I told her that for the sake of her unborn baby, she had best try not to get too upset."

"Did your sister call you before she attempted suicide?"

"Not right before. She knew I'd try to stop her somehow if I knew about it. None of us in the family ever thought she'd shoot herself, but just a couple of months after her daughter was born, that's just what she did."

"How did your family feel about Morgan Simmons after Ina shot herself?"

"Thought he was dirt," she said. "We tried to tell Ina that she deserved better, but she wouldn't listen to us. She was still crazy over him. When he promised to treat her right, like a dang fool, she took him right back."

"Did he treat her better?"

"He appeared to for a few years. Then, about two years ago, we started hearing tales about him being seen with some woman."

"Did you tell your sister about these rumors?"

"No. None of us wanted to upset her. She still looked poorly from her operations, and we didn't want to get her all torn up without proof."

"You say she looked poorly. Do you mean she had lost weight, or looked ill?"

"She never did gain back the weight she'd lost after the surgery. She always had a tired look in her eyes."

"Did your sister tell you how she learned about the other woman her husband had been seeing?"

"Yes. She called me up right after that Miss Owens called her on the phone. Said the woman had the nerve to tell her to give Morgan the message that she didn't want to see him for Christmas."

"What did you say to your sister after she had told you about the call?"

"I told her she should come live with me and leave Morgan Simmons without leaving so much as a note of goodbye. It's bad enough for somebody's husband to cheat on them, but nothing could be worse than having the other woman smear your face in it that way."

"Did your sister accept your invitation to come live with you?"

"No. She said she had to stay with him for the children's sake and hoped he would stop seeing that woman. I knew she still loved him, though, and it seemed like nothing he did to her was going to change that."

"Did your sister tell you about meeting with, talking with, or seeing Miss Owens?"

"Yes. She told me the woman called and talked to her in Morgan's office. Miss Owens told her she'd slept in her bed with Morgan while Ina was in the hospital in Lexington. And Ina told me about meeting Miss Owens and seeing all the fine things Morgan had bought for the whore."

"Objection!" Sandusky was red-faced with anger. "I demand an end to this name-calling of the deceased."

"She's just callin' her what she was!" an anonymous woman shouted from somewhere in the audience. Several people applauded the statement, and a "That's right!" chorus chimed in from various points in the crowded hall.

"Order in the court!" Judge Tartar said. Mumbling soon gave way to silence, then Tartar sustained Sandusky's objection. "The witness will cease to use derogatory names to refer to Miss Owens. And one more outburst like the last one from the audience and I will have this courtroom emptied of all spectators."

Pope turned back toward the witness.

"In other words, Mrs. Barton, you were a constant witness to your sister's humiliation at the hands of her husband and Miss Owens?"

"Yes, I was."

"How would you describe your sister's mental and physical condition the last time you saw her, before the incident on the train?"

"I went to see her along about the last week of July. She told me Morgan had been treating her better. He never would talk about Miss Owens or the times he had spent with her, but at least he was staying home at night. I figure that made Ina hope he would change."

"Are you saying that she had recovered from her emotional problems?"

"No. She was still nervous over what she'd been through. She told me she wished she had enough money to buy a house and get some new clothes for her girls."

"Did your sister call you before she got on the train that day in August, or tell you anything about a plan to harm Miss Owens or her husband?"

"No. I was shocked when I heard about what had happened."

"Would you describe your sister as a violent person?"

"No. She is a kind, giving person. She has always been willing to do anything for her family and her friends. I don't think she's ever hurt a soul on purpose. It ain't like my sister to do what they said she did on that train. Up till then, Ina'd only hurt herself by staying with Morgan. He put her through hell. I don't see how she stood Morgan Simmons for as long as she did."

"I have no further questions for this witness," Pope said.

"State's witness," Judge Tartar said.

"Mrs. Barton, I understand it's your contention that your sister remained married to Morgan Simmons despite your pleas to get her to leave him because she had a deep and abiding love for him, a love that enabled her to forgive his unfaithfulness to her on more than one occasion," Sandusky said.

"Yes, that's the way I always seen it,"

"Why do you think your sister shot herself approximately six years ago?"

"I believe she was so confused, she didn't know what else to do to try to keep him."

"Then, you don't believe she really intended to kill herself? She hoped that she would finally get her husband's attention, and that he would treat her and her children with the respect they deserved?"

"I don't know if Ina even knows that for sure. I know how much she loves her babies, and I don't think she would have meant for them to be raised without her. Then again, none of us can really know what she was thinking, or how confused she might have been when she shot herself. I only know she must of been hurting awfully bad."

"Do you feel your sister's suicide attempt can be looked at as an indicator of how much she loved her husband, and how desperate she was to regain his love?"

"I might say that. Then again, I might say it showed how much he had messed up her mind by not being true to her."

"And since you say she might have shot herself in an effort to keep his love, do you think her husband might have convinced her to kill Miss Owens—if it was the only way he could remain by her side and stay out of prison for embezzlement?"

"Objection," Pope said. "Calls for speculation on the part of the witness."

"I'll allow it," Judge Tartar said.

"I think that's stretching it a might far. My sister would have to have been completely out of her mind to allow Morgan to talk her into such a thing. No mother in her right mind would take a chance of being separated from her babies and going to the electric chair for a no-good man like Morgan Simmons."

"You say he was no good, but love will often make a person do strange things, won't it, Mrs. Barton?"

"Sometimes, it can."

"But didn't she take a terrible chance of being permanently taken from her children when she attempted to kill herself? Hasn't your sister taken two terrible chances because she loved her husband enough to do anything for him?"

"I don't think there's any proof of that!"

"But the circumstances of this murder do make one wonder, don't they, Mrs. Barton?" Sandusky asked rhetorically. "I have no further questions for the witness."

Judge Tartar excused Mrs. Barton, and the defense called Miss Helen Jensen of Whitley City. The tall teenager, with long, straight blonde hair, dressed in a blue cotton dress with a bow tied around the waist, took the stand.

"Miss Jensen, are you acquainted with Mrs. Ina Simmons?" Pope asked.

"Y—yes,"

Pope noticed the girl's tension and said, "Take a deep breath, honey. It's ok to be a little nervous."

She paused, exhaled deeply, took a breath, and then continued.

"We lived cross the street from her in Whitley City—before they was burned out."

"Did you ever, on any occasion, see another woman in the Simmons household when Mrs. Simmons was not at home?"

"Yes, I met another woman in their house last February, while Mrs. Simmons was in the hospital in Lexington . . ."

Helen stood shivering in the winter chill outside Morgan Simmons' door with a picnic basket in her hands. After she had waited patiently for what seemed like several minutes for a response to her knock, Morgan finally cracked the door open to greet her.

"Helen, what a surprise!" He was afraid his nervousness showed. "Are you here to play with the girls?"

The girl looked past Morgan, and stared into the living room at an unfamiliar woman sitting on the couch with the Simmons children.

"No," Helen replied, holding up the wicker picnic basket. "Momma told Mrs. Simmons before she left that I'd look in on your young'uns while she was away. Momma thought you might like some hot food, what with men folk not being too good in the kitchen and all."

"Your momma's got that right," Morgan strained to appear jovial. He knew the teenager had already caught a glimpse of Pearl.

"It's mighty cold, Helen. Won't you come in?" he asked.

Helen accepted his invitation, and he closed the door quickly behind her.

"Helen, I would like you to meet Mrs.—Vaughn. She's an old friend of Ina's. She's come to help me with the girls while their mother's away."

Pearl stood to offer her hand in greeting to Helen. The girl stood star struck for a moment until she realized she was staring. She had never seen such a beautiful, stunningly dressed woman before, except in the movies. Pearl's makeup, clothing, pearl necklace, and diamond rings set her apart from all the other women in Whitley City . . .

"Did you believe this woman was a friend of Mrs. Simmons?" Pope asked.

"It didn't seem quite right to me, but I couldn't say nothin' about it to him." The girl twirled a lock of hair over her right ear.

"Of course you couldn't. Did you ever mention to Mrs. Simmons that you had seen a woman in her house while she was away?"

"I thought maybe I should, but Daddy said it wasn't none of our business. He said the kids would probably tell her anyway."

"Did the children talk to you about this 'Mrs. Vaughn' at any time?"

"Yes, whilst I was laying the picnic basket on the table, Melissa, Mrs. Simmons' oldest girl, asked me if I thought Mrs. Vaughn was pretty. She said she thought Mrs. Vaughn was beautiful, that she had never seed such pretty clothes and jewelry before."

"Then it was your impression that this "Mrs. Vaughn" had gained the affection of Mrs. Simmons' children?"

"Yes."

"Did you see this woman who called herself Mrs. Vaughn on any other occasion?"

"No. Not until I seen a picture of her in the newspaper. The paper called her Miss Owens, and said she had been killed on the train."

"Thank you, Miss Jensen. I have no further questions for the witness, your honor," Pope said.

"State's witness," Tartar said.

"Miss Jensen, while you were in the Simmons house, or at any other time, did you ever see Mr. Simmons embrace, kiss, or show any form of affection towards this Mrs. Vaughn?" Sandusky asked.

"No, I didn't."

"And did the children ever tell you later that they had seen any improper form of affection displayed between their father and Mrs. Vaughn?"

"No, they didn't."

"I have no further questions for this witness, your honor," Sandusky said.

Judge Tartar excused Helen Jensen, and the defense called Mrs. George Jensen. A tall woman of stout build, dressed in a blue polka dot dress and wearing her black hair in a bun, took the stand.

"Mrs. Jensen, I understand that you are the mother of the last witness, Miss Helen Jensen," Pope said.

"I am."

"What did your daughter tell you that evening after she left the picnic basket at the Simmons house?"

"She said there was some fancy-looking woman named Mrs. Vaughn over there who claimed to be a friend of Mrs. Simmons."

"Did you find it unusual that such a woman would be visiting the Simmons household?"

"I certainly did. I'd never seen a woman fitting that description call on the Simmons house. Of course, I'd heard people talk about Mr. Simmons having a thing for the ladies."

"So you were suspicious about this woman's intentions?"

"Especially when I didn't see her leave the house that night. I saw her pass by the window a couple of times after Morgan left for work the next day."

"I see that you are quite observant, Mrs. Jensen," Pope grinned. Several members of the audience chuckled at the remark.

"It pays a body to be these days." Mrs. Jensen's smile indicated she had accepted Pope's statement as a compliment.

"Thank you, Mrs. Jensen. I have no further questions," Pope said.

"State's witness," the judge said.

"Mrs. Jensen, did you actually meet the woman your daughter told you about in the Simmons house?" Sandusky asked.

"No, I didn't."

"How far was it from the front porch of your house to the living room window of the Simmons house?"

"A hundred feet, maybe? I'm afraid I'm not very good with distances."

"And you never saw this woman from a closer distance?"

"No, I didn't."

"Then you can't be sure this woman was Miss Owens, can you? After all, you said you never actually met her or saw her up close."

"No, but she had dark hair, like the woman in the newspaper pictures."

"But it could have been another dark-haired woman that you saw the next day in the house, couldn't it?"

"I suppose it could have been."

"I have no further questions for this witness, your honor," Sandusky said.

Judge Tartar excused Mrs. Jensen, and Pope called Henry Vance to the stand. A tall, gaunt old man dressed in baggy black slacks and a dingy white shirt, with the long sleeves rolled above both elbows, was sworn in.

"Mr. Vance, what is your occupation?" Pope asked.

Vance contemplated a chunk of dried clay on the toe of one of his worn boots as he responded, "I'm the desk clerk at the Whitley City Hotel."

He had told Pope last week that he didn't feel comfortable about appearing in court, and "couldn't see as I can do Mrs. Simmons' case much good," but the attorney had insisted upon the value of his testimony, then thanked him in advance with a plug of his favorite chewing tobacco.

"Did Mrs. Simmons ever stay at your hotel?"

"Yes, she and her family moved in last March, after their house burned."

"How would you describe Mrs. Simmons while she lived at the hotel?"

"She was always nervous. Looked peaked most of the time, like she didn't get much sleep."

"Did you know the Simmons family before they moved into the hotel?"

"Sure did. Whitley City is a little place. Most folks knows everybody else. I've seen Mrs. Simmons on the streets downtown for, oh, the last five or six years."

"Did her physical appearance change any during those years?"

"She looked skinnier every time I seen her."

"Did you know her husband very well?"

"No, he was a quiet sort. Never said much, less you said something to him first."

"Would you say that he was affectionate towards his wife?"

"Never seen him hold her hand, make over her, or nothing like that. He walked beside of her, but like I said, he never said too much."

"I have no further questions for the witness," Pope said.

"State's witness," Tartar said.

"Mr. Vance, did Mrs. Simmons ever tell you that she was on a diet?" Sandusky asked.

"Course not. That weren't none of my business." Vance stifled the urge to start chewing on a small, fresh chunk of tobacco nestled between his upper left cheek and gum.

"Did she ever tell you that she had any kind of illness, or discuss any of her problems with you?"

"No. Mrs. Simmons was a proper lady at all times. Just cause she stayed in my hotel don't mean she told me her business."

"No, it doesn't. Thank you, Mr. Vance. I have no further questions, your honor," Sandusky said.

Henry Vance was excused, and Pope called Frank Lester of Pine Knot, Kentucky. Lester, a tall, middle-aged man with greying temples, stood, sucked in his slightly rounded stomach, buttoned the bottom button of his vest, and took the stand.

"Mr. Lester, what is your occupation?"

"I was sheriff of McCreary County—up till the last election. Now, I guess you can say that I'm retired."

"When you were sheriff, did you have occasion to meet Mrs. Ina Simmons and her husband?"

"Many times. I worked out of the courthouse in Whitley City every day. Mr. Simmons was the county court clerk, and Ina was his chief deputy."

"How often did she visit the courthouse?"

"It varied. She was supposed to come in if Mr. Simmons was out of town or needed her help."

"Did you ever see Mr. Simmons with a woman other than his wife?"

"At the courthouse, you mean?"

"Yes, at the courthouse."

"I don't think he was with anybody in particular, but I seen him flirt with lots of the gals in the courthouse. Mr. Simmons was a real charmer around the ladies. He always had a line to make them laugh."

"Did you consider his actions improper?"

"I don't think his missus would have been none too happy. Course, lots of fellas will bend a lady's ear, if'n they get the chance." Lester raised his eyebrows playfully. Several members of the audience laughed at the gesture.

"Thank you, Mr. Lester," Pope said. "I have no further questions."

"State's witness," Judge Tartar said.

"Mr. Lester," Sandusky began in a slow, solemn tone, "did you ever see Mr. Simmons kiss any of the women in the courthouse, or make any public displays of affection towards them?"

"No. He may have patted one of them on the shoulder, but he never did nothing nobody would get flustered about."

"In other words, you just considered Mr. Simmons' interactions with the women to be nothing more than office camaraderie?"

"That's right. Just a little joshing 'tween office workers. Nothing to it."

"I have no further questions for the witness," Sandusky said.

Judge Tartar excused the witness, and the defense called Mrs. Arthur Dewey. A plump, middle-aged woman, richly dressed in a black dress and matching black felt hat, took the witness stand.

"Mrs. Dewey, where were you on the night of August 9, 1928?" Pope asked.

"I was coming home from Louisville on the southbound Southern Railway train. I used to live there, you know."

"No, I didn't know that, Mrs. Dewey," Pope said. "Where were you seated on the train?"

"Next to the window." She anticipated Pope's next question, pointed toward Ina at the defense's table, and said, "Mrs. Simmons there was sitting in the aisle seat on the row behind me."

"When did you first become aware of Mrs. Simmons?"

"Not until after the train had pulled out of the Somerset station. I just happened to glance back over my right shoulder, for no particular reason, when I saw her."

"Was there anything specific you remember about her appearance?"

"The pretty hat she was wearing. Then, I noticed her expression. She looked very troubled, as if something very bad had happened."

"Did you see what might have distressed her?"

"No. I turned back around. I didn't want to be rude and stare at her."

"Did you see Mrs. Simmons again that night on the train?"

"No. Not until after the commotion. After the train stopped, I saw the conductor trying to calm her down. She was going on something awful."

"You mean she was emotionally upset—crying?"

"Yes. She was a nervous wreck."

"I have no further questions for the witness," Pope said.

"State's witness," the judge said.

"Mrs. Dewey, did you happen to see a man and woman sitting together in the aisle across from Mrs. Simmons?" Sandusky asked.

"No. The train was crowded that night. I'm afraid nothing stands out about anyone else."

"Thank you, Mrs. Dewey. I have no further questions, your honor."

"The defense calls Dan Dean," Pope said.

"Mr. Dean, we understand from your previous testimony that you were the conductor on duty in the coach in which the shooting occurred on the night of August 9, 1928."

"That's right."

"Could you describe Mrs. Simmons' condition when you saw her after the train had stopped?"

"John Heinz, the flagman, was already beside her, trying to calm her down. She was resting her head on the back of the chair in front of her, and looking down into her lap as she cried."

"She was very upset then?"

"Yes, I'd say highly upset. She got even worse when we tried to calm her."

"Did she say anything, or seem to realize what had happened?"

"I don't recollect her saying anything. She just wailed, like some folks do at funerals."

"Did she have a gun in her hands?"

"No. There was a pistol on the seat to her right. I picked it up, and later on I handed it to A. C. Snyder, the roundhouse foreman at Ferguson."

"Thank you for clarifying this point for us, Mr. Dean. Mr. Snyder was unsure whether it was you or Mr. Heinz who gave the gun to him. At any time, did you see Mrs. Simmons touch the gun?"

"No. The first time I noticed it, it was sitting on the seat."

"No further questions, your honor," Pope said.

"State's witness," Judge Tartar said.

"Mr. Dean," Sandusky said, "you indicated in earlier testimony that you saw a hatbox near Mrs. Simmons?"

"Yes, there was a empty one on the floor in front of the seat where I found the gun."

"Was there any paper, cloth, or other packing material present in the hatbox?"

"No. I'm sure there was nothing inside."

"Thank you, Mr. Dean. I have no further questions, your honor."

After Judge Tartar excused Dean, the defense called Major S.S. Morrow to the stand. "Maj," as Morrow was affectionately known about town, was the brother of former Kentucky Governor Ed Morrow and Mrs. Simmons' defense attorney, W. Boyd Morrow. After being sworn in, Maj unbuttoned his black suit coat before sitting down.

"Major Morrow, what is your occupation?" Pope asked.

"I'm the captain for railway police in this region."

"Major Morrow, did you see Mrs. Simmons of the night of August 9, 1928?"

"Yes. Mrs. Simmons was still seated on the train when I arrived on the scene."

"Could you describe her condition at the moment of your arrival?"

"She seemed to be in shock. The conductor, Mr. Dean, was trying to talk to her, but she didn't seem to hear a word he was saying."

"Did you hear her respond to any of his questions?"

"No. I don't think she ever answered him."

"Did you ask her any questions?"

"No. Patrolman Matney came in about that time, so I let him question her."

"Did she answer any questions for him?"

"No. He told her she was under arrest, and she got hysterical at that point, started crying uncontrollably."

"Did you follow her and the patrolman outside the coach?"

"No. I stayed inside to examine the scene of the crime and interview the conductor. He, and later Mr. Heinz, was able to provide me with the information I needed to file my reports for the railroad."

"I have no further questions for the witness," Pope said.

"State's witness," the judge said.

"Major Morrow," Sandusky asked, "when you examined the scene of the murder, did you happen to notice a hatbox anywhere near Mrs. Simmons' seat?"

"Yes. There was an open hatbox on the floor of the seat next to her."

"Did you have any theories about the empty hatbox?"

"Not at the time. It occurred to me later that if Mrs. Simmons had been wearing the hat, she might have been carrying the pistol in it."

"That is what we have heard Mrs. Simmons testify. Did you notice any packing material in the bottom of the box which might have been used to prevent a pistol from sliding about?"

"No. It was empty."

"As it would have been if it had been used to carry a hat like the one Mrs. Simmons was wearing upon her head?"

"Yes."

"She was still wearing a hat when you saw her?"

"Yes. She was, as I recall."

"In your opinion, would someone carrying a gun in a hatbox carry it without any sort of padding material?"

"No. Not if they wanted to keep it from banging around inside the box."

Pope stood and said, "Your honor, I fail to see the importance of all this hatbox questioning."

"Your honor," Sandusky said, "I'm merely trying to remind the jury that Mrs. Simmons has stated that she has been acquainted with guns since childhood, and someone so acquainted probably would have taken precautions in their handling and transport. Since no one saw evidence in the hatbox of such measures, I believe it casts serious doubts on Mrs. Simmons' claim that she carried the murder weapon in the hatbox."

"Objection withdrawn, your honor," Pope reclaimed his chair, upset he had provided Sandusky with the opportunity to elaborate on his point.

"You may resume your examination," Judge Tartar said.

"I have no further questions for the witness, your honor," Sandusky said.

Major Morrow was excused, and the state called Somerset Police patrolman McKinley Matney. Matney took the stand, then removed his cap and carefully placed it on his lap.

"Mr. Matney, what was Mrs. Simmons' condition when you first saw her on the train?" Pope asked.

"She was crying and rocking backwards and forwards in her seat."

"Did you ask her any questions?"

"Yeah, but she didn't answer me. I told her she was under arrest, suspicion of murder, then she took to screamin'."

"You were unable to get any answers to your questions?"

"She wouldn't in no condition to answer. She buckled in the knees as I fixed to take her out of the coach. I was afraid she was going to collapse before I could get her into Chief Warren's car."

"Would it be fair to say that Mrs. Simmons appeared to be grief-stricken during the time you spent with her?" Pope asked.

"Objection!" Sandusky said. "Neither the patrolman, or anyone else for that matter, can say whether Mrs. Simmons was experiencing grief over what she had done."

Judge Tartar sustained.

"I have no further questions for the witness," Pope said.

"State's witness," Tartar said.

"I have no questions for the witness," Sandusky said.

Patrolman Matney was excused, and the defense called Wester Kamen. A short, stocky man dressed in a new pair of blue overalls took the stand.

"Mr. Kamen, what is your occupation?" Pope asked.

"I'm a machinist at the Ferguson roundhouse."

"Did you see Mrs. Ina Simmons on the night of August 9, 1928?"

"Yes. I heard what had happened. Like most of the men, I left my post to see what was going on. I was standing along the tracks at the entrance to the coach when the patrolman brung Mrs. Simmons out."

"How would you describe her condition?"

"She was plumb pitiful, a going on something terrible. I think she was hollerin' for somebody."

"Do you remember what she said?"

"She said, 'I want my babies and Morgan' or something to that effect."

"Did anyone come when she called?"

"No, but I could see the patrolman was having a hard time with her. It looked like she couldn't stand, so I helped him get her down the steps and into Chief Warren's car."

"Thank you, Mr. Kamen. I have no further questions," Pope said.

"State's witness," Tartar said.

"I have no questions for the witness, your honor," Sandusky said.

After Wester Kamen was excused, the defense called C. I. Ross of Somerset. Ross, wearing a black pinstripe suit and red bow tie, took the stand.

"Mr. Ross, I understand that you are the circuit clerk here in the Somerset courthouse, and that Mrs. Simmons was brought before you immediately after the incident on the train," Pope said.

"That is correct."

"How would you describe Mrs. Simmons' general physical condition at that time?"

"The poor woman was on the verge of collapse. Her eyes was bloodshot, and she sobbed the entire time she was in my office."

"Was she responsive?"

"Barely. I asked her if she realized she had been arrested. She said she did, but she didn't remember doing anything wrong."

"Where did Mrs. Simmons go after leaving your office?"

"Chief Warren wanted her placed in Somerset General for observation."

"Do you think that was a wise decision?"

"Yes. I don't think she would have stood up to any questioning, the shape she was in."

"I have no further questions for the witness," Pope said.

"State's witness," Tartar said.

"I have no questions for this witness, your honor," Sandusky said.

"Your honor," Pope said, "Mr. Ross was our last witness. The defense rests its case."

Judge Tartar breathed a visible sigh of relief, then glanced at his watch. "Gentlemen, it's now 8:35. I will begin preparing my instructions to the jury. We will hear your closing arguments tomorrow. Court is adjourned until 9 a.m."

After a drop of the judge's gavel, the mass of tired spectators and the trial participants exited the courtroom.

CHAPTER 17

By 7 a.m. on Saturday, February 16, 1929, hundreds of spectators had again gathered outside the Somerset Courthouse. Everyone knew that this would be the final day of the drama, the day that the attorneys would render their closing statements and Judge Tartar would place Ina Mae Simmons' fate in the jury's hands.

Security was especially tight after the gun-drawing incident of the day before. Police Chief Warren had been hailed as a hero in the morning papers for averting a potential tragedy in the courtroom on Friday. This morning, he and his officers, as well as officers of the court, kept a close watch on everyone who entered the courtroom, and examined the contents of all purses and coats.

As on previous days, all the seats in the audience section were soon filled, as well as the window ledges, aisles, doorways, and spaces along the four walls. In order to fit as many citizens as possible into the courthouse, Chief Warren again allowed spectators to cross the railing which divided the audience from the judge and attorney area. When that area was filled, spectators were allowed to sit on the railing. Before 9 a.m., every available inch of floor space was occupied, and spectators were again perched on Judge Tartar's platform.

When Ina and her entourage of relatives and attorneys entered from the anteroom, everyone in the audience stood at attention. The bailiff announced Judge Tartar. The judge dropped his gavel, and court was called to order.

"Before we get started today," Judge Tartar said, "I want to ask the jury if anyone among them has seen or heard any of the recent news stories which have been written about this trial."

One elderly man in the jury raised his hand and said, "I have, your honor. This morning I happened to read part of a article in *The Louisville*

Herald-Post. I was half-way into it 'fore I 'membered I weren't 'pose to be readin' the papers."

"Do you believe anything which you read will have prejudiced or swayed you in any way for or against the defendant?" Tartar asked.

"No, your honor. I don't reckon it had no effect on me one way or t'other."

"Does counsel for the defense or the prosecution object to the continued presence of this juror on the panel?" Tartar asked.

"I've read the article in question and found nothing objectionable in its content," Pope said.

"Neither did I, your honor," Sandusky said.

"Very well," Judge Tartar said. "I hereby instruct the officers of this court to prevent all members of the jury from securing newspapers for the remainder of this trial. We have come too far to risk a mistrial."

"Your honor, before we continue, the defense would like to submit a paragraph for inclusion in your instructions to the jury." Pope handed a type-written sheet to the judge.

Judge Tartar accepted the page and silently read its content: "If you shall believe from the evidence in this case, that at the time the defendant shot and killed the deceased, Pearl Owens, and if you shall believe from the evidence that she did do so, and that the said Ina Simmons was actuated by an uncontrollable impulse to such an extent that she did not know or realize the consequence of her act in firing that shot, and by reasons of said insane impulse she did not have sufficient will power to govern her actions, then and in that event you will find her not guilty." The judge paused for a moment to consider the statement, then spoke.

"Mr. Pope, I've carefully considered your proposed amendment to the instructions to the jury. However, I don't consider some of the wording suitable."

"But your honor, the defense respectfully feels it is vital that an allowance be made for the uncontrollable impulse."

"When I deliver the instructions, the defense will see I've made allowances for the consideration of the plea of emotional insanity," Tartar said.

"Your honor, since we are on this topic, the state also objects to the testimony offered by defense witnesses supporting the validity of an 'insane impulse,'" Sandusky said. "Since none of the distinguished physicians were present at the moment the crime was committed, this so-called insane impulse is nothing more than a hypothesis the defense has cooked up to keep their client out of the electric chair."

"Objection, your honor!" Pope said. "The defense has not 'cooked up' anything. All of the members of the medical profession who testified yesterday are experts in their respective fields. Their testimony as to Mrs.

Simmons' probable mental condition at the time of the tragedy is certainly valid."

"Gentlemen," Tartar said, "I see this discussion is going to become much more heated and involved. Since this is not the place for such a conversation, I request that counsel for the state and the defense accompany me to my chambers in order that we might come to an agreement on this matter."

Before the last attorney had entered the judge's chambers, Sandusky started making his point to Tartar.

"Roscoe, the only 'insane impulse' worth talking about is the one the defense had when they decided to drag this team of doctors into the courthouse. There's no way anybody, doctors included, can say Ina Simmons acted on impulse."

"They didn't say she definitely did," Pope said. "They testified as to her probable mental condition. That's quite a different thing."

"But how likely is the jury to make that distinction?" Sandusky asked.

"I can see your point, J.S.," Tartar said, "but you know it's academic to disregard the physicians' testimony at this point. The jury has heard what they've heard, and it's not likely that anything I can say about disregarding testimony will make them forget it. It's up to you, in your closing statement, to convince the jury to disbelieve this insane impulse business. I'm going to allow the doctors' testimony to stand."

"Thank you, your honor," Pope said.

"Your honor," Kennedy said, "defense respectfully requests a clarification on the instructions on manslaughter."

"I told Mr. Pope the jury's instructions will include ample consideration of the emotional stability of the accused; therefore, I have no intention of changing instructions along the lines of defense's proposal.

"As you are well aware from your tenure in this robe, Mr. Kennedy, the burden of proving insanity is always on the defense's shoulders. I will remind the jury that the accused is always considered sane unless proved otherwise."

"Very well, your honor," Kennedy said.

"If there's nothing further, gentlemen, let's continue with the trial," Tartar said.

Judge Tartar and the attorneys returned to the courtroom, and the judge began reading his instructions to the jury.

"Gentlemen of the jury, you have heard the evidence in this trial. Momentarily, you will hear the closing arguments of the defense and the prosecution. Listen closely as I read the seven following options upon which you will deliberate as to the innocence or the guilt of the accused, Ina Mae Simmons.

"Number 1. The words "willfully" and "willful" as used in these instructions, mean intentionally, not accidental or voluntary. The word "feloniously" as used in these instructions means proceeding from an evil heart or purpose, done with the deliberate intention of committing a crime. The words "malice aforethought" as used in these instructions mean a predetermination to commit the act of killing without legal excuse, and it is immaterial at what time before the killing such a determination was formed.

"Number 2. If the jury believe from the evidence beyond a reasonable doubt that the defendant Ina Simmons, in Pulaski County, and before the finding of the indictment, did willfully, feloniously, and of her malice aforethought, and not in her necessary or reasonably apparent necessary self defense, shoot and kill Pearl Owens, you should find her guilty of willful murder as charged in the indictment and fix her punishment at death or confinement in the State Penitentiary for life in your discretion.

"Number 3. Although the jury may not believe from the evidence beyond a reasonable doubt that the defendant Ina Simmons has been proven guilty of willful murder as defined in instruction #2, but shall believe from the evidence beyond a reasonable doubt that she did in Pulaski County and before the finding of the indictment, without previous malice and not in her necessary or reasonably apparent necessary self-defense, but in sudden affray or in sudden heat and passion upon provocation reasonably calculated to excite her passions beyond the power of her self-control, shoot and kill Pearl Owens, you should in that event find her guilty of voluntary manslaughter, and fix her punishment at confinement in the State Penitentiary for a period of not less than two nor more than twenty-one years in your discretion.

"Number 4. If you shall believe from the evidence beyond a reasonable doubt that the defendant has been proven guilty either of willful murder as defined by instruction #2, or of voluntary manslaughter as defined by instruction #3, but shall have a reasonable doubt from all the evidence as to whether the defendant be guilty of willful murder or of voluntary manslaughter, then it will be your duty to find her guilty of the lower offense, voluntary manslaughter.

"Number 5. If you believe from the evidence that at the time the defendant Ina Simmons shot and killed Pearl Owens, that she was without sufficient mind or reason to know what she was doing, or that she had not sufficient mind or reason to know right from wrong or that as a result of mental unsoundness she had not then sufficient will power to govern her actions by reason of some insane impulse which she could not resist and control, then in that event you will find the defendant not guilty.

"Number 6. The law presumes however, that every person is sane until the contrary is shown by the evidence and before the defendant can be excused or acquitted on the ground of insanity, you must believe from the evidence that the defendant, at the time of the killing of Pearl Owens, was without sufficient mind or reason to know what she was doing, or that she had not sufficient mind or reason to know right from wrong, or that as a result of mental unsoundness she had not then sufficient will power to govern her actions by reason of some insane impulse which she could not resist or control.

"Number 7. If upon the whole case the jury have a reasonable doubt from all the evidence of the defendant having been proven guilty by the evidence, you will find her not guilty.

"Again, I will remind the jury that the law presumes a person as sane unless proven otherwise. Gentlemen, these are the points upon which you will deliberate after hearing the closing arguments of the defense and the prosecution. A copy of these points will be provided for your deliberations. A maximum of two hours will be allowed for each side to present their summation. The court will now hear the closing arguments of the defense."

"Your honor," Pope said, "the closing arguments for the defense will be delivered by me and Mr. H. C. Kennedy."

"So noted. Please proceed, Mr. Pope."

Pope rose from his chair and walked slowly toward the jury. He looked at each of their faces for a moment, and then began.

"This is the case of a gingham girl, with her head wrapped in a towel, charged with killing a scarlet woman in glittering gold and sparkling diamonds, arrayed like Solomon in all his glory by the girl's husband, who denied his wife and babies the necessities of life that he might retain the affections of the Louisville woman.

"This is also a case which forces us to examine the question of right and virtue versus prostitution and crime. You see before you the virtuous mother of two lovely little girls. This woman has been married for ten years to a man who doesn't deserve her love or the love of her children, but for the good of her children, and in the hope of preserving their home, Mrs. Simmons tried repeatedly to hold onto the love of her husband.

"This was not an easy thing for her to do. As Mrs. Simmons and other witnesses have testified, Pearl Owens did everything in her power to rob Ina Simmons of the affections of her own husband. That sparkling city woman relentlessly stalked Morgan Simmons, and even desecrated this poor woman's home while she was struggling to keep her sanity in a Lexington hospital.

"On more than one occasion, Ina Simmons pleaded with her faithless husband, 'Please come back to me and our babies. Please be my husband, and love only me and your little ones.' " Pope spoke in a pitiful tone, which had an immediate impact on the jury. One elderly juror bent over and placed his head in his hands. His back trembled as he silently wept. Handkerchiefs were drawn across the audience, and many people sobbed.

Gerald Griffin, local reporter and correspondent for *The Louisville Herald-*

Courier, would later report that at one point fully half of the jurors were in tears, and even the stern police chief, Robert "Moster" Warren, was seen brushing a tear from the tip of his nose.

Pope continued, "And what did Morgan Simmons do? He enjoyed Miss Owens illicit affections so much that he repeatedly abandoned his own wife and children. While they sat at home, alone, unprotected and wearing ragged, second-hand clothes, he was with Pearl Owens in hotels across Kentucky, buying her fine things with his wife and babies' insurance money and the funds he had stolen from the people of his home county who had trusted him enough to elect him to office.

"Pearl Owens successfully usurped Mrs. Simmons in Morgan Simmons' affections, but was that enough for that wicked woman? Oh no. On one occasion of their meeting, Pearl Owens flaunted in Mrs. Simmons' face diamonds, silks, and furs bought with insurance money resulting from the fire which destroyed Mrs. Simmons' home. For years, Pearl Owens inflicted the most severe form of torture upon Ina Simmons—torture of the heart," Pope said, making a clutching motion at his breast, "and of the body and soul.

"As a series of well-respected physicians have told you, Mrs. Simmons paid a heavy price for the torment Pearl Owens and Morgan Simmons cruelly inflicted upon her. She experienced a severe loss of weight, and found it nearly impossible to enjoy the peace of a good night's sleep. Day and night, her nerves left her in a frayed, weakened condition. It was in this condition that she boarded the train to Danville. It was in this demoralized condition that she allegedly shot Pearl Owens.

"Gentlemen, if Ina Simmons did indeed shoot Pearl Owens, she was justified in doing so. That woman had made life a living hell for this frail woman. This poor lass from the hills wanted nothing more out of life than to raise her two babies in a good, loving home, but Pearl Owens had so devastated Ina Simmons that she could scarcely function as a mother to these two little ones." Pope's voice trembled and tears welled in his eyes as he gestured toward Ina and her daughters.

Tears ran down Ina's cheeks as Pope spoke. Her children, their eyes red from crying, held tight to her dress and leaned against her for comfort.

"That Louisville woman prostituted her affections in exchange for diamonds and furs, while Ina Simmons repeatedly, freely offered her husband the pure love of her heart, but he repeatedly turned her and his children away for Mrs. Owens' immoral love.

"In courtrooms across this land, men have killed to preserve the dignity and honor of their wives and children. Yes, this is often referred to as 'the unwritten law,' and no, it is not admissible as a legal defense. But it has been considered by many juries as a moral defense. Men have been set free for killing in defense of their families and their homes. Women are entitled to receive the same consideration as men in relation to this moral defense. Ina Simmons may have slain Pearl Owens while in the grip of an insane impulse, but if she did so, it was in defense of her babies and her home.

"If Ina Simmons did fire those two shots into Pearl Owens, one shot was wasted, and that shot was the one that should have snuffed out the life of Mrs. Simmons' errant husband, who made the life of his children's mother a 'little hell' here on earth. It was Mr. Simmons who ran like a guilty man when Pearl Owens was killed.

"Gentlemen of the jury, I want to remind you that no one came forth during this trial to testify that they saw Ina Simmons with that gun in her hand. For all we know, it might have been Morgan Simmons who committed this murder. After all, he might have had the motive to kill his lover. Perhaps, as the prosecution has proposed, Mr. Simmons had grown tired of Miss Owens. Maybe he was afraid she would tell about the vast sums of money he had spent on jewels and furs for her. Maybe she would have testified that Mr. Simmons had embezzled that money from the people of McCreary County.

"And let us consider Mrs. Simmons' previous history of mental problems which Morgan Simmons visited upon his poor wife more than six years ago. At that time, his infidelities so depressed this good woman that she tried to take her own life. Morgan Simmons knew that his wife had been in and out of hospitals and doctors' offices all across the state of Kentucky. He knew that a case could be made that his wife was a crazy person. After all, a person would have to be crazy to shoot another person in the back of the head right in public, wouldn't they?"

Pope paused for a moment to allow the jury time for contemplation. "That's what Morgan Simmons might have been thinking if he actually pulled the trigger. He knew it would be so easy to blame it on his poor wife. I believe that is what has been done here.

"The Commonwealth has failed to introduce one shred of evidence to prove that Mrs. Simmons fired those fatal shots; therefore, there is more than reasonable doubt that this little woman is guilty of murder. Gentlemen of the jury, you have the power to place the electrodes of death on the head of Ina Simmons and send her to the electric chair. Or you can crown her with freedom that she might rear her two children in the paths of rectitude and right." Again, Pope paused for effect, then said solemnly, "Gentlemen, the power is in your hands."

Pope turned from the jury and walked back to his table. He had spoken for one hour and fifteen minutes of the defense's allotted time. H.C. Kennedy stood and replaced Pope in front of the jurors.

Kennedy, known for his fiery method of delivery, began to speak, with a booming voice that carried to all corners of the crowded courtroom.

"Gentlemen, you have heard my colleagues and the honorable judge speak about emotional insanity and the unwritten law. Having spent some time on the bench myself, I feel qualified to explain to you that these two concepts are not one and the same. As Mr. Pope has explained so eloquently, the unwritten law is so called because it is not written down in any law books. If anything, it is a recognition of numerous juries across this country that there are often moral considerations which go beyond the laws which men have written down. One of these moral considerations is that no man or woman should break apart a family and its members. Anyone who dares to break apart a family may find themselves subjected to the rightful anger of the harmed party.

"That is what we are talking about in this case. Pearl Owens did everything she could to take Ina Simmons' husband from his loving wife and children. At the same time, Miss Owens was selling her affections for worldly goods—"

"Objection!" Sandusky said. "There is no evidence that Miss Owens was guilty of any immoral activity."

"Sustained," Judge Tartar said. "The jury will ignore that last comment."

"Ina Simmons was kind and loving towards her husband during the time he was unfaithful to her. She tried to win her husband's love, and at no time is there any evidence that she wished her rival any physical harm."

Kennedy slipped his thumbs under the straps of his black suspenders at the waist and paced slowly back and forth before the jury.

"This brings us to the point of emotional insanity. From the start of this case, the defense has admitted that the evidence would lead one to believe that Mrs. Simmons is guilty of the murder of Pearl Owens. While we are uncertain who actually fired the fatal shots, we know that Ina Simmons might have done so had she been emotionally insane at the instant she saw Pearl Owens and her husband embracing on that train.

"As we have heard in the testimony of respected physicians, Mrs. Simmons was the perfect candidate for an insane episode. For years, her physical and mental health were in decline. This decline was brought on primarily by her husband's infidelities, but the loss of her home and all her possessions, as well as her family's humiliation, brought about by her husband's indictment for criminal activities, helped push this poor woman over the edge. As her doctors have all told you, she probably was seized by an insane impulse on that train. Her most primitive emotions took control of her brain, and she lashed out in an unthinking way. In the respected opinions of her physicians, she cannot be held accountable for actions which may have occurred while she was bereft of her will of control . . ."

Kennedy paused to roll the sleeves of his white shirt above the elbows, and then continued.

"Now that I've explained emotional insanity, I want to tell you what this

119

case has really been about. This case is more than a defense of Ina Simmons. What we are really defending today is chastity and womanhood of the nation. Mrs. Simmons represents all that is good, wholesome, virtuous, and pure in our country. She is a good Christian woman whose lifelong ambition has been to be the best wife and mother that she could possibly be. All her life, she has been taught that it is honorable to be faithful and true to one man, and that one man should be her husband.

"Gentlemen, Mrs. Simmons' upbringing is the kind that made America what it is today. Where would we be without women like her who have gladly made it their life's work to provide a happy home for their husbands and their children? I shudder to think of what the alternative offers us.

"Pearl Owens represents what that alternative offers. We have all heard about the new breed of woman that is coming forth in our nation's large, sinful cities. They say these women smoke and drink like the worst of men. They stay out all night and fornicate with any man who catches their fancy. Unfortunately, there are married men out there looking for this new kind of woman, and their wives and children are left at home to suffer for their infidelities.

"What will become of the children of this nation if their fathers all start abandoning them for these serpents of the night? Pearl Owens was a married woman, until she decided that she wanted to be a little more like the worst of men. She wanted to leave her child at home while she went looking for the evil pleasures of the night.

"Miss Owens was divorced because she had these desires. While one of her sisters cared for her little boy, Pearl Owens lived the life of the serpent. She tempted Morgan Simmons with the forbidden fruit of her body, and Morgan Simmons welcomed her into his heart and into the home he unworthily shared with his wife and two babies.

"She turned what should have been a paradise into a life of living hell for Mrs. Simmons. She asked for diamonds and furs, and Morgan Simmons complied. In reality, Pearl Owens' demands denied Mrs. Simmons and her children the fruits of paradise. Without the money to replace what they had lost, this woman and her children were turned out, near-naked and hungry, into the uncaring outside world."

Kennedy raised his right hand above his head, pointed his index finger toward the ceiling, and proclaimed, "In a moment of uncharacteristic rage, Mrs. Simmons did what the Bible commands us to do—to bruise the head of the serpent with our heel. Even then, she did what she did to preserve her family. What she did, she did out of love for her children and their undeserving father."

Jurors and spectators alike were comforted by the style of Kennedy's appeal; he made them feel as if they were sitting in the pews of a church listening to a preacher deliver his Sunday sermon.

"I'm certain that Mrs. Simmons would much prefer to go to the electric chair if the jury believes her guilty than to spend several years or a lifetime behind the cold walls of a penitentiary," Kennedy said emphatically. "That electric chair would at least grant her the peace of death, and an end to the torment that Pearl Owens brought upon her.

"Imagine what life would be like for Mrs. Simmons behind those prison walls. Sitting in that tiny prison cell, she would know her babies were growing up without her guidance, without all the loving care that she felt born to give to them. Day after day, night after night, she would rock back and forth, crying out, 'Melissa and Gloria, how are you my dear ones? Please, God, let me be with them!' "

Kennedy wringed his hands, and tears glistened in his eyes as he repeated the imagined plea. Again, several jurors sobbed and wiped at their eyes with handkerchiefs.

"I beg of you, gentlemen of the jury, to render a verdict in favor of the home. Do your part to reward faithful women and mothers across this land. Send them a message that the serpent will be kept outside their doors. Send this good mother back to her children. Let her raise them in the ways of virtue. Do not entrust these little ones to a father that will leave them alone at night in their beds while he consorts with the serpents of the night."

H. C. Kennedy returned to his chair. Judge Tartar said, "It's now 12:05. We will recess until 1:00 for lunch. When we return, we will hear the state's closing arguments."

As before, many people opted to remain in their seats and eat bag lunches. Those who did leave the courthouse did not stray far, hoping to reclaim their seats when the trial resumed.

Howard Denton nervously picked through a light lunch with Sandusky and Shadoan. Shadoan offered moral support to the rookie attorney, which was easy for him to do. Sandusky had delegated little responsibility to Shadoan during the trial, who was primarily standing by in case either of the other two attorneys should take ill. Sandusky assured young Denton that he would do fine, and that he had a world of faith that he would be able to more than uphold his end of the closing.

Still, minutes later, Howard felt a bit weak in the knees as he approached the jury. This was, after all, his first closing argument in a murder trial. He had listened closely to all the testimony and arguments, and taken a notepad full of notes in the last few days. He had several important points to make—if he could remain calm in the spotlight.

When he opened his mouth, the words came easily, and he realized his fears were unwarranted.

"Your honor, Mr. Sandusky and I will be delivering the state's closing argument," Denton said.

"So noted," Tartar replied.

Denton took a deep breath, and then turned to face the jury.

"Gentlemen, you must not let the defense distract you from the true issue in this case. Attorney Morrow opened with an effort to cloud the issue. He said this case would open the lives of three people up for examination, but we have only heard about the life of the accused and the way she perceived Miss Pearl Owens and her own husband, Morgan Simmons.

"Mr. Simmons has chosen, as is his right under the law, not to testify for or against his wife; therefore, we cannot examine his perspective of events. Obviously, Miss Owens is unable to verify or contest anything because she was brutally murdered and has been resting in her grave since last August. That fact is what this case is about.

"Miss Pearl Decker Owens was brutally murdered on a southbound train on the night of August 9, 1928. She was shot in the back of the head from behind without a single word of warning or provocation. Her killer did not slay in self-defense, and all indications are the victim did not even know her murderer was on the train. There is not even any proof that Miss Owens ever actually met or spoke with Ina Simmons.

"Sure, Mrs. Simmons has told us about talking with Miss Owens on the phone a couple of times, and about seeing her in person twice before she shot her, but there is no one to verify that these conversations or meetings actually took place.

"The defense has tried to make it seem that Miss Pearl Owens has been on trial here, that she had stolen something from Mrs. Simmons which merited her execution. Miss Owens did not take anything which belonged to Mrs. Simmons. Mrs. Simmons has presented proof that her husband wrote two checks totaling a mere $70 to Miss Owens. Mrs. Simmons has alleged that her husband bought expensive clothing and jewelry for Miss Owens, but she has not produced a single receipt as proof.

"The defense would have you believe that Miss Owens had stolen away the affections of Mr. Simmons in the same way that someone might steal a watch or some other treasured possession. Only an immature individual could believe that affection is something which can be stolen. If Mr. Simmons did endow Miss Owens with any affection or material possessions, it was entirely because he freely chose to do so.

"True, he was the husband of another, but he was not a possession, like a piece of livestock, that belonged to his wife. Infidelity is a terrible thing, but if Mr. Simmons chose to be unfaithful to his wife, that was his own decision. Pearl Owens did not take anything which was not given to her. Pearl Decker Owens did not deserve to be brutally murdered in cold blood because someone believed she had taken someone from them . . .

"Miss Owens has been spoken of as a city woman, a scarlet woman, a woman who sparkled with jewelry. She has been referred to as an abstraction, a thing which represents a new, destructive kind of woman. She was none of these things. Pearl Decker Owens was a living, breathing, dreaming human being, like all of us here in this courtroom.

"She had three brothers and four sisters. She was unhappily married, but before that marriage ended, she gave birth to a son. His name is Robert. He is seven years old, and for the rest of his life, he will not have a mother to hold him and to love him. Think of him when you deliberate this case. Think of what you will say to him if he comes to you one day and asks if you saw justice done in the slaying of his mother.

"Yes, Miss Owens was a divorced woman, but that does not mean she was a leper or an outcast; she is only one of many more we will see in the future. It's true that people are different in the big cities, and women are starting to enter into areas formerly inhabited almost exclusively by men, but we in the rural towns and villages must not judge their lives to be wrong because they differ from ours.

"Judge not lest ye be judged, the Good Book says, and the jury must not enter into deliberations with the intention of judging the perceived morality of Pearl Decker Owens. Instead, you must determine the guilt or innocence of the woman who ended her life, and as the defense admits, all the evidence in this case points toward Ina Simmons.

"The defense has implied that the evidence is not strong enough to convict their client, but they know that it is. That is why they have tried to distract you with a plea of the unwritten law. Gentlemen, have you ever wondered why the unwritten law isn't a written law? If it's such a universally-agreed-upon good thing, shouldn't it have been written down somewhere, and allowances made for it, the same way allowances have been made for emotional insanity? There is no unwritten law to consider in this case. As Mrs. Simmons' attorneys use the term, it's another excuse to try to save their client from the electric chair.

"Make no mistake about it—there is a moral issue in this case. A woman was shot down without warning in the prime of her life. That is the moral issue we should concentrate on here.

"The defense has added a plea of emotional insanity to a plea based on a non-existent law. Therefore, their only plea, then, is emotional insanity. It all comes down to this: can we believe Mrs. Simmons was emotionally insane at the moment she pulled the trigger and killed Miss Owens?

"The defense has presented four physicians, some of whom had not seen Mrs. Simmons in recent years, who were not even present on the train when the shooting occurred, yet they say they can state with certainty that their former patient must have been seized by 'an insane impulse' which rendered her unable to control her actions. I find it highly unlikely that their diagnosis is accurate. My doctor always insists I come into his office for a checkup, and I doubt he could be very effective over the telephone."

Denton grinned slightly, but no one in the courtroom gave any indication that they appreciated his sarcastic humor.

Denton turned toward Ina and her attorneys and said, "I don't believe Mrs. Simmons ever gave a satisfactory explanation about how she knew to go to Danville, or why she believed her husband would meet Pearl in Somerset. She would have us believe she was guided by a hunch to travel to Danville, and by pure chance, she 'happened' to see Pearl Owens waiting to board a southbound train.

"She would have us believe she suspected her husband would meet Pearl Owens late that night somewhere south of Danville. Surely, she didn't expect them to meet in Somerset? Mrs. Simmons has told us about the fake telegram calling her husband to Somerset, so there was no reason for her to expect her husband to be in Somerset.

"Gentlemen of the jury, I interviewed the operator who was on duty the day Mrs. Simmons alleges she confronted a telegraph operator about a message calling Mr. Simmons to Somerset. The operator stated that she didn't remember seeing either Mr. or Mrs. Simmons on that day, and that she would never risk her job by falsifying messages for anyone. I'm sure Mrs. Simmons' attorneys questioned the telegraph operator and were told the same thing; otherwise, she would have been subpoenaed to testify in this courtroom.

"I don't believe there was a faked message, but there probably was a message calling Mr. Simmons to Somerset. As Morgan Simmons told the newspapers, he had spent the day in this town on business, and he did board the train here on the night of August 9, 1928. Either Mrs. Simmons, Mr. Simmons, or a combination of both, concocted this story about a fake message to provide a justification for Mrs. Simmons' suspicion that Pearl Owens was still involved with her husband.

"Ina Simmons would have us believe that she borrowed a hat and matching outfit because her own clothing was not suitable to wear in public, yet she supposedly went to Lexington in June and July last year without the benefit of borrowed clothing. Apparently, her own clothing was good enough on those occasions, but when she borrowed clothing from Miss Williams, she did so because she needed a disguise.

"Ina Simmons claims she carried one of her husband's pistols with her as a routine matter of protection, but I think you and I know differently. If she did get on that train at Stearns with a gun in the borrowed hatbox, she did so with the intention of using it on Miss Owens. She rode that train north from Stearns to Danville, a distance of 76 miles by rail, and she sat near Miss Owens for 44 miles on a southbound train before she twice pulled that trigger. I would say that Mrs. Simmons had plenty of time to consider her actions, and that her disguise and preparedness were the premeditated actions of a clear-headed individual.

"She may have been strained by the loss of her home, but there is no evidence in the McCreary County Courthouse to support her allegation that her husband has been indicted on embezzlement charges."

The audience grumbled at this revelation; they refused to consider that Mrs. Simmons might have lied about the indictment during her testimony.

Spectators in the front row looked to Pope for his reaction. His face had suddenly reddened. Someone should have verified Ina's statement about the indictment. Boyd coached her—he should have seen to this, but Pope was the one with the egg on his face.

The judge pounded his gavel to squelch the multitude of conversations that erupted across the courtroom.

"I think it's clear what we have here. This is a case of premeditated murder. The evidence points toward the guilt, rather than the emotional insanity, of Mrs. Ina Simmons. The state asks that Mrs. Simmons be given the death penalty for the brutal, premeditated murder of Miss Pearl Decker Owens," he concluded.

Denton returned to the prosecution table. J. S. Sandusky gave his young colleague a nod for a job well done, then the elder attorney took his turn before the jury.

As Sandusky began to speak, his face was red and his voice louder than it had been at any point in the trial.

"This is the unfairest trial I have ever gone through, due in large part to the unfair tactics of the defense and the sacrilegious remarks of Mr. Morrow and those of the Pope of Knoxville," Sandusky roared, pointing toward the defense table.

"Objection!" Kennedy said. "I object to the unfair and discourteous remarks of the state's attorney. That is a religious slur against my respected colleague."

"Overruled," Judge Tartar said.

Pope steamed in his chair, outraged at what he perceived as Judge Tartar's inability to recognize that Sandusky was trying to play upon the possible anti-Catholic sensitivities of the predominantly Baptist jury.

Sandusky continued, "This entire trial has been carried out in an atmosphere resembling a carnival or a sporting event. The newspapers across this state have attempted to try this case long before a jury was selected, and I wonder, after the admission of the juror today, if anyone anywhere could totally avoid the trial publicity.

"What we should all be concerned with is obtaining justice. The murder of Pearl Decker Owens was a diabolical plot between Mrs. Simmons and her husband to get rid of Pearl Owens. Since all the evidence points toward Mrs. Simmons, she should be punished for her crime.

"As you will remember, Mrs. Simmons claims she carried the murder weapon in her hatbox. I don't believe Mrs. Simmons carried her pistol in the hatbox. There was no packing material in the bottom of the hatbox, as I believe there would have been if an experienced gun-handler like Mrs. Simmons had really transported a gun in it. I believe when Morgan Simmons got on the train in Somerset, he placed the pistol in his wife's hands—"

Sandusky's theory remained unpopular with the crowd, and again, the audience voiced its disapproval across the courtroom. As Judge Tartar pounded his gavel for order, Sandusky continued, shouting over the mumbled conversations.

"After his wife did the deed, he pursued Mrs. Owens' body to the funeral home, and before her body was even cold, he slipped the rings from her lifeless fingers.

"Mrs. Simmons was supposed to be the individual on trial here, but instead I've heard the name of the murdered woman slandered in the most revolting ways. The Pope of Knoxville, in his holier-than-thou statements, has called the late Miss Owens a scarlet woman and other vile—"

"Objection!" Kennedy said. "Mr. Sandusky is again—"

Before Kennedy could finish registering his complaint, Judge Tartar said, "Overruled."

"The defense should be ashamed for its lack of respect for the dead. It has failed to prove that Miss Owens was a scarlet or immoral woman. It has failed to produce evidence that Miss Owens received enormous sums of money from Mr. Simmons, and it has failed to substantiate Mrs. Simmons' allegations that her husband has been indicted on embezzlement charges. It has failed to produce the telegraph operator who Mrs. Simmons alleges falsified a telegram calling her husband to Somerset.

"It has failed to prove that Mrs. Simmons ever met or spoke with Miss Owens, or that Miss Owens had her arms around Mr. Simmons when she was brutally murdered. The defense has failed to prove that Mrs. Simmons was emotionally disturbed or insane at the moment she slew Miss Owens. All the evidence points toward a calculated plan to murder Miss Pearl Owens.

"The only thing which the Pope has—"

"Your honor," Kennedy said, "how many times must—"

"Overruled," Tartar said, again cutting Kennedy off.

"The Pope," Sandusky repeated, "and his colleagues have succeeded in sacrilegiously defaming the name and reputation of a dead woman, a woman whose only known crime was being acquainted with and sitting in a seat beside the husband of the woman who killed her in cold blood. Gentlemen of the jury, if justice is to be done, you must sentence Ina Mae Simmons to death in the electric chair."

It was 3:15 when Sandusky returned to his chair at the prosecution table.

"Gentlemen of the jury," Judge Tartar said, "you have now heard all the evidence in this case. Do not be hasty in your deliberations. Murder is the most serious crime which can be committed in our society. The bailiff will now direct you to the anteroom."

As the jury marched out, Judge Tartar cautioned the huge audience, "I expect no demonstrations in this courtroom when the verdict is returned. Anyone acting disruptively will be charged with contempt of court and jailed immediately."

CHAPTER 18

After ten minutes, tension began to show on the faces of Ina and her family. Her father gripped her right hand reassuringly while her oldest daughter massaged her neck.

In the front row of chairs along the railing, reporter Elbert Raney of *The Louisville Times* turned to Gerald Griffin of *The Courier Journal* and asked, "Do you think we'll be in for a long wait?"

"No," Griffin replied. "Matter of fact, I'm surprised it's taken this long. In my experience with trials around here, five minutes is about average."

"They must be taking the judge's comments to heart about not making any hasty decisions."

"Appears so. I don't . . . Look—Sandusky is putting on his coat and hat."

"Mr. Sandusky," Raney said, "where are you headed? Aren't you going to wait to see how it turns out?"

Sandusky turned and said, "I don't have much doubt about the outcome. I'm heading back home to Monticello."

"How about you and Mr. Shadoan?" Griffin asked Howard Denton.

"We'll be here. We don't have any other plans," Denton said.

At 3:40, ten minutes after Sandusky exited the courthouse, the door to the anteroom opened, and a hush traveled through the audience as the bailiff led the jury back into the courtroom. As the jurors walked in, Ina nervously twisted a button on her dark blue dress and leaned forward to listen for the verdict.

After the twelve men returned to their swivel chairs, Judge Tartar said, "I want to commend the audience for their patience during the jury's deliberations. I ask that you continue to exhibit such good behavior after the verdict is read, regardless of the decision. Now, gentlemen, have you reached a verdict?"

Foreman J. M. Burke stood and said, "We have your honor." He turned through the three pages of the copy of the judge's instructions to the jury which had been used to record the verdict. He fumbled past page two, where a check mark had been placed by option no. 7. Ina's father, sister, and brothers crowded close against her as they awaited the verdict.

After what seemed like minutes to Ina, foreman Burke arrived at his hand-scribbled note on page three. He looked from the paper to the judge.

Judge Tartar broke the oppressive silence. "Read your verdict."

Foreman Burke smiled, then read the words, "We, the jury, find the defendant not guilty."

A cacophony of cheers, whistles, and handclaps erupted in the courtroom. Judge Tartar pounded his gavel for order, but the overjoyed crowd ignored his pleas. A middle-aged woman sitting on Ina's side of the railing reached her before Ina's own sister could offer her congratulations. The woman embraced Ina and kissed her on the lips.

Then, as Ina attempted to rise from her chair, her sister kissed her. Ina's daughters tugged at her dress, but she brushed them aside, and with tears streaming down her cheeks, she almost ran to the jurors. She thanked each juror and shook their hand.

Hundreds of men and women began elbowing their way toward the railing to offer their congratulations to Ina. Ina's children, terrified by the chaos, clung tightly to their mother's dress. Police Chief Warren and Patrolman McKinley Matney waded through the crowd on Ina's side of the railing to stand guard by her.

"Mrs. Simmons," Gerald Griffin shouted, "do you have a statement for the press?"

"I was never so happy in my whole life," Mrs. Simmons said, "and it's the first time in a long time that I could say I was happy and glad." Ina's eyes sparkled as she spoke. It was the first time since the opening of the trial on Wednesday morning that she had not been in or on the verge of tears.

Ina, accompanied by Chief Warren and Patrolman Matney, walked to the railing to receive the adoring throng of well-wishers. A line formed, and practically every person in the room marched by, in what resembled a White House reception, to touch Ina's hand and offer their congratulations. To each well-wisher she said, "Thank you."

When the room cleared, Ina left the courthouse. Accompanied by an honor guard of policemen and a crowd of more than 300 spectators, Ina walked across the public square toward the Newtonian Hotel. As she crossed the square, her husband. Morgan, stared at her from his seat on the porch of the hotel, but Ina gave no indication that she had seen him.

Gerald Griffin noticed Morgan and asked him for a statement.

"I haven't anything to say," Morgan said. "Of course, you can say that I'm mighty glad Mrs. Simmons was acquitted, and I'm happy for her."

Before entering the ladies entrance to the Newtonian, Ina stopped with her team of attorneys for a few final questions from the press.

"Mrs. Simmons," Elbert Raney asked, "did you ever have any doubt about what the outcome would be?"

"No," Ina replied. "I had total faith in my fine attorneys."

"How about you, Mr. Pope?" Griffin asked.

"I never entertained any doubt that my client would be found not guilty. The jury's verdict was a reward for a virtuous woman and chaste living."

"Mrs. Simmons, what are your plans?" Raney asked.

"I'm going to have supper with my family, and then accompany my brother back to Corbin for a visit at his home."

Ina's sister tugged at her arm, and they disappeared through the hotel's ladies entrance.

"I'm afraid my girl's been through too much today for any more questions, gentlemen," Ina's father said. "I'm shore she'll be glad to talk later."

At 5:30 that afternoon, Ina and her brother left in his car, headed toward Corbin, Kentucky. Morgan started to approach the vehicle before it pulled away from the hotel, but because a large crowd was looking on, he decided to forego his plans to bid Ina farewell.

CHAPTER 19

On Monday morning, February 18, a reporter for *The Louisville Times* tracked Ina down a muddy dirt road in Corbin for a follow-up story. Ina invited the reporter to sit with her at the kitchen table to conduct the interview.

"Mrs. Simmons, what are your plans for the future?" the reporter asked.

"This is the happiest moment of my life, and I want to take the time to enjoy it. After I relax for a couple of weeks, I expect to seek a position as stenographer and give my children an education." Ina smiled.

"Do you have any plans to reunite with your husband?"

"I don't plan to return to my husband, but I do forgive him for his unfaithfulness to me. He stood by me throughout the trial and assisted me and my attorneys in every way possible. It would be unfair if I didn't show appreciation of this."

"Have you recovered from the strain of the trial?"

"Yes. There were some tense moments. I was confident the jury would find me not guilty." She paused for a moment, and then added, "But you can't always tell what a jury of twelve men will do."

"Do you have a special message that you'd like to send our readers?"

"I want the world to know how much I appreciate the way the people of Pulaski and surrounding counties stood by me from the beginning. They are the most wonderful people I ever met. When the jury brought in the verdict, I felt so good I wanted to hug every one of those precious men. I shook the hands of each one, and they cried for me. It just seemed as if I had wings and wanted to fly away. I felt sure they would find me not guilty when they heard my story."

"How long do you plan to stay in Corbin?"

"I'll be going back to my father's house in Junction City about the middle of this week. Then I'll visit some of my relatives in Tennessee for a week. After that, I'll go looking for a job."

"Where are your children?"

"They're with my mom and dad in Junction City. They're starting school there today. I felt we needed a change from Whitley City."

The reporter thanked Ina for the interview, and on the way back to Louisville, he stopped in Whitley City to interview Morgan Simmons, who had returned to his job as clerk of the circuit court in the McCreary County courthouse.

"Mr. Simmons, do you have any plans to reconcile with your wife?" the reporter asked from a chair on the opposite side of Morgan's desk.

"No. I haven't considered going back to her," Morgan said. He nervously tapped a pencil on his desk.

"What are your plans for the future?"

"Nothing definite. I expect to continue here in my clerk's position until the end of my term. And then, who knows? I'll just take things as they come."

"What about your children, Mr. Simmons? Have you seen them since the trial?"

"No, but I plan to, real soon. They've been through an awful lot," he said. "I'd like to make it up to them if I can. I hope they're young enough to forget and get on with their lives. That's all any of us can do."

End

AFTERWORD

About two months after the not-guilty verdict, Morgan and Ina Simmons were reunited. The couple and their two children moved back to Whitley City, where Mr. Simmons bought the Whitley City Hotel. They lived there for a time before moving to Florida.

The family prospered; Morgan Simmons provided a cook and a maid for the household, and according to a family friend I interviewed in 1991, he was the model husband and father. His two daughters, the only children from the marriage, were still living in 1991, and, in the words of the family friend, "have always cherished the memory of their mother and father."

In 1939, while living in Florida, Morgan suffered a fatal heart attack. His wife and children returned to the area, and Mr. Simmons was buried in Whitley City. His wife met and married a funeral home director from Danville, Kentucky, the town where her fateful southbound train ride began on August 9, 1928. Ina and her second husband lived for the remainder of their lives in Danville. According to the family friend, Ina "lost her mind" in the last years of her life, and passed away in 1980.

Pearl Decker Owens' only son, Robert, lived in Harmontown, Mississippi with his mother's sister, Annie Freeman, and her husband, Hermie. Annie died in 1932, and her husband continued to raise his adopted son. Robert had completed one year at Mississippi State College in Starkville, when he was stricken with a streptococci infection. He died at age 18 and was buried in Harmontown.

On July 9, 1991, I visited Nell Pulliam, the only surviving member of Pearl's immediate family, in the Louisville Masonic Home for Widows. Mrs. Pulliam, remarkably unwrinkled for her nearly 90 years, was unfortunately unable to remember much about her sister, who she described as "very beautiful." She said that even when Pearl was very young, men would tip their hats to her on the street.

When I asked her about the jewelry her sister was supposedly wearing at the time of her death, she said, "I don't know nothing about that. Never heard nothing about it." She did say she had heard that the woman who shot Pearl had told her to leave her husband alone, but Pearl had always been very stubborn, and would never take anyone's advice. She couldn't remember anything else at all about her sister, and ended our interview by saying, "Write anything that you like."

A daughter of Pearl's brother, Claude Decker, said her only information about Pearl was that "she was too pretty for her own good, and it got her killed." She also had heard that Pearl had been married to a man who had dearly loved her, but had been unable to provide her with all the things she wanted.

No actual transcript exists of the trial, but copies of the indictment, instructions to the jury (and its handwritten verdict), court docket, and court orders were obtained from the Kentucky Department of Library and Archives in Frankfort in the summer of 1991.

Most of the old records from counties in Kentucky are stored in the Archives, but the records for McCreary County are still stored in its courthouse in Whitley City. As attorney Howard Denton states in the narrative, there is no record of any indictment against the presiding clerk of the circuit court in 1928.